JoLyn

many successes!

Jon
Yoons

Praise for Jen Groover

"Jen has something special about her; her passion and creativity are infectious. She has the soul of an entrepreneur and it radiates off her—and she proves it every day. Jen's book is the perfect extension to teach others how to create their own success."

—Donny Deutsch

"Jen Groover is not only an innovative entrepreneur, she is the expert people listen to when it comes to understanding their business, their brand, and their vision of their own future. *What If? & Why Not?* provides readers with the much-sought-after success formula Jen uses to continuing pushing the limits of each and every idea. Her interviews, tips, lessons, and life story inspire you to dream big and achieve even bigger."

—Tamsen Fadal, News Anchor, TV Show Host, and Author of *Why Hasn't He Called?*

"Look no further for inspiration—for any entrepreneur looking for guidance and [his or her] own personal cheering section, Jen Groover is it! Jen Groover is quite simply the most motivating woman I've ever met."

—Amy Palmer, Emmy-Nominated TV Host and Producer and Founder of PowerwomenTV

"Jen Groover is the epitome of a role model to women young and old, which she shows by conducting herself with endless energy, optimism, and inspiration. At the same time, she proves herself as the quintessential businesswoman by trailblazing her way to the top of a business that is dominated by men."

—Judy Goss, Bookings and Castings Editor at *More* Magazine

"Jen Groover is a go-to guest when it comes to segments focusing on entrepreneurs and small business expertise. Groover combines expert knowledge based on her amazing track record with a great personality that viewers love."

—Mike Straka, Executive Producer of FOX News' *The Strategy Room*

"As an innovator and product developer, Jen is the true meaning of a 'one-woman brand.' She has learned to dream big and then make her dreams a reality. She also takes the time to help and inspire the people around her so that they too may follow their true passion in life. To describe Jen in one word is not possible, but if I had to, that word would be: inspiration."

—Dianna Feldman, Founder of TopButton.com and TheTopSecret.com

"From the moment I met Jen, I knew I was face-to-face with an incredibly creative and bright woman who has what it takes to become a cultural icon for today's entrepreneur. I never ceased to be amazed at her many projects and her passion for living life. With all she has already accomplished, I suspect that this is still only just the beginning for Jen!"

—Joel Comm, *New York Times* Bestselling Author and
Executive Producer of *The Next Internet Millionaire*

"Jen Groover is an inspiration! Jen's intelligence, ambition, and tenacity rate high in this world. She stops at nothing in going after her goals. Not only has Jen set high goals for herself, she has definitely identified success in this marketplace. But I believe what has led Jen to her success is what she possesses inside. Her genuine and heartfelt personality has allowed her to catapult quickly to the top. In my line of work I meet people every day and Jen truly stands out. She has learned a lot in her lifetime and has taken what she has learned and makes it work for her every day. Needless to say I am a big fan, follower, and believer in Jen Groover."

—Sheila Conlin, President of The Conlin Company,
Casting Director for *Hell's Kitchen* and *Secret Millionaire*

"Creative powerhouse, highly energetic, generous, and kind . . . just a few words I would use to describe inventor and entrepreneur extraordinaire Jen Groover. From her innovative Butler Bag to her ability to develop products in any area, we just watch in awe as she continues her upward ascent."

—Victoria Colligan, Co-Founder, Ladies Who Launch

"Jen Groover is in a league of her own. She's an inspiration to everyone trying to find the best in life. At home and in business, Jen projects a positive and innovative lifestyle, motivating thousands of women and men who seek success. It is a joy being around her as she is a major asset to any business project as well as any discussion or strategy session in general."

—Mort Fleischner, Former Executive Producer of *ABC Nightly News*
and *Good Morning America*

"Jen isn't just a fresh drink of water, she's a fire hydrant. Though I've only known her a short while, I'm nonetheless impressed by her drive, vision, and entrepreneurial spirit."

—David W. Dunham, The Dunham Group, Inc.

"Jen has the confidence, drive, and the ability to bring the very best out of everyone she touches. She educates, enlightens, and inspires. Watch out Martha Stewart. There's a new woman in town!"

—Jess Todtfeld, President of Media Training Worldwide, Executive Producer of
The Speaking Channel, and Ex-Producer of FOX News

What If? & Why Not?

How to Transform Your Fears Into Action and Start the Business of Your Dreams

Jen Groover

BENBELLA BOOKS, INC.
Dallas, TX

BenBella Books, Inc.
6440 N. Central Expressway, Suite 503
Dallas, TX 75206
www.benbellabooks.com
Send feedback to feedback@benbellabooks.com

Printed in the United States of America
10 9 8 7 6 5 4 3 2 1

Library of Congress Cataloging-in-Publication Data is available for this title.
ISBN 978-1-935251-67-5

Copyediting by Rebecca Logan
Proofreading by Erica Lovett and Gregory Teague
Cover design by The DesignWorks Group
Text design and composition by PerfecType, Nashville, TN
Printed by Bang Printing

Distributed by Perseus Distribution
perseusdistribution.com

To place orders through Perseus Distribution:
Tel: (800) 343-4499
Fax: (800) 351-5073
E-mail: orderentry@perseusbooks.com

Significant discounts for bulk sales are available. Please contact Glenn Yeffeth at glenn@benbellabooks.com or (214) 750-3628.

Contents

Introduction

Some men see things as they are and say, "Why?" I dream dreams that never were and say, "Why not?"

—George Bernard Shaw

Baseball and football are two of the top American pastimes. I sometimes think a third is telling people all the reasons they can't do something. It's like there's a National Dream Surveillance System that, as soon as you announce your passion for becoming a jazz musician, running for office, or starting your own business, gives you reasons why you can't follow your dream. You would think we would know better. This is a country built by entrepreneurs and daring people with crazy ideas: Benjamin Franklin, Thomas Edison, Henry Ford, and many, many more. This is a world that thrives on entrepreneurship, so I find it disheartening that we are not more supportive culturally, educationally, and financially of people who want to defy convention, promote innovations, start their own companies, and make the world a better place. These people should be the true rock stars of our culture.

In my life as a businesswoman and entrepreneur, I have come up against many of the obstacles I write about in this book. As someone who dreams of launching your own small business, you have probably encountered them yourself. If you have, you have learned something I also realized years ago: although many of those obstacles are out of your control, the most dangerous ones are those that exist only inside your head. They are the fears and doubts that hit when you look at the task ahead of you and think, "That's a wall I'll never be able to climb." I'm here to tell you that you can climb it. With every wall you climb, you get better at it.

But you must first be willing to face and take on the fears and doubts rather than let them become an excuse for setting your great idea on the shelf and saying, "Someday." No. Someday is today. If you have a terrific business idea but you've reached that point where you're telling yourself those energy-draining lies—"I don't know what I'm doing" or "I will never be successful at this"—it's time to turn that thinking around. Time to face the possibility of failure and think, "You know, I might just succeed!" Because in reality, the only way you fail as an entrepreneur is to not take action at all.

Confessions of a Bag Lady

I can say this because I've been there many times. I've had the flash of inspiration and then heard people telling me, "Jen, it'll never work." I've had to climb my personal walls while carrying a lot of baggage. Most people think when they meet me, with my outgoing personality, I must have been class president with a charmed life. But that's just not true. I wasn't great in school. I talked too much. I got A-plusses in Socializing 101 but barely got by in everything else. Today, even members of my family look at what I've done and think, "How on earth did *that* happen?" My childhood, like many, had many challenges, and I was an extremely independent teenager with my own set of obstacles. So believe me, if you're feeling lost or powerless, I know exactly what you're feeling, because I have been there.

To thrive, I had to develop a self-taught philosophy of positive thinking, and it really began to pay off in 2006. I was a businesswoman and the mother of beautiful twin girls, but I was irritated at never being able to find what I needed in my handbag. Then came the moment that every entrepreneur knows so well: the Big Idea. One night as I was doing the dishes, I saw how all the utensils were standing up straight in the dishwasher's silverware tray and realized that's how I wanted my handbag to be organized. I slid the silverware tray out of the dishwasher and thought, "That would be a perfect thing for organizing a woman's purse." I slipped it into one of my handbags, and other women saw it and said, "That's a fantastic idea! I would love to have my bag organized like that!" This inspired me to move forward with my dream, and an empire was born. I asked myself, "What if my idea has real value and my potential for success is enormous?" and, "Why not bring it to fruition and see what happens?" I knew I didn't want any more regrets in my life.

So in just a few years, faster than anyone imagined possible, I've launched one of the fastest-growing fashion accessory and lifestyle brands, through the Butler Bag Company. I've created accessories, children's products, products for parents, and TV show concepts; appeared all over television and the print media; and started selling Jen Groover–branded merchandise through retailers like QVC, Kmart, AVON, and Target. I've also coached thousands of budding entrepreneurs like you in how to overcome mental, organizational, and financial challenges to get their dream off the ground. I've started LaunchersCafe.com to enable new entrepreneurs to connect and find the resources they need. I've done what you're dying to do, and I didn't know what I was doing when I started, either.

However, although my success has been gratifying and new opportunities continue to come along at an incredible pace, it hasn't been easy. I've made mistakes. There's not a successful business mogul, entrepreneur, or self-employed person out there who hasn't. Every time I try to expand my vision into a new area of business, I run into new walls and obstacles. And that's okay. In fact, I welcome it. Failing and overcoming obstacles is how we learn, and we get better when we learn to move through those moments.

Learning the Hard Way

My education began early: as soon as I created the Butler Bag, I was faced with the immediate challenge of finding a factory to produce the first line. I had been a professional fitness trainer and fitness competitor, so I knew next to nothing about the accessories industry. The learning curve came quickly. A good friend referred me to a reputable manufacturer, and I assumed that after some negotiations and discussions of design and fabrication specs, the first Butler Bags would soon be rolling off the assembly line. Wow, don't I wish.

Nine months later, the factory had produced excuses and headaches but not a single bag. Retailers who wanted to carry it had no choice but to dedicate store space to something else. I had made the mistake of not doing my due diligence and chosen a manufacturer that also made its own line of retail products, so its own products got priority. I was left—you should pardon the expression—holding the bag. When I finally did get the bags—from a different manufacturer, no less—they were wrong, and I had to eat the cost. I'd spent eighteen months struggling just to get to that point only to see all my work come to nothing.

This was devastating emotionally and financially. It would have been easy to blame the manufacturer, but it had been my choice. The failure was my responsibility. A new business is like a newborn child—it's very fragile. If I had made my failure personal and felt sorry for myself, the Butler Bag and all my dreams would have ended then and there. At first, I did feel like giving up; who wouldn't? I started to question my own abilities and if I even belonged in this business. I had a lot of sleepless nights (and still have them). But in the end, I made a different decision. I asked myself, "What if I used this experience to fine-tune my ability to evaluate companies?" In seeking another manufacturer to turn out the Butler Bag, I remembered that harsh lesson and did my due diligence, and this time things went as planned.

As a result of that early catastrophe, I've learned to align myself with incredible companies and individuals who have helped me develop my best ideas. My learning curve might have been much longer—and the damage to my business interests greater—had I not learned from that priceless failure early on. The key was that I chose to see the episode as an invaluable chance to develop keener judgment and learn from my mistake. If I had started down the road of saying self-defeating things like, "I just don't know enough about this business," I would have been done. Because I was able to rethink a negative experience, I turned what could have been a dead end into a speed bump.

Asking the Right Questions

This is a book about overcoming self-doubt and the fear of failure so that you can take action to bring your entrepreneurial dream to life. I have found that this leads to many other personal dreams coming to life as well, because starting a business is about more than making a living. It's about the fulfillment of your creative spirit and personal vision. It's about pushing yourself constantly to live up to your full potential. That's why the hardest part of getting started and sustaining your business is overcoming your own thinking.

Yes, there are external challenges when you're trying to start a business: funding, competition, product development, hiring, and so on. But what really matters is whether you believe you have the ability to face and overcome those challenges. **Until you can jump over your inner roadblocks, the outer ones will stay firmly in place.** Overcoming these inner obstacles is about learning to rethink the fearful thoughts that can lead you to quit before you start. It's about changing your mind-set. This is the crucial tipping point that will allow you to unlock the door to what you *deserve*. I have found that many people don't pursue their dreams because they don't feel that they deserve them. But what if you do? As Penn State football coach Joe Paterno says, "Believe deep down in your heart that you are destined to do great things." I believe we all are—that each and every one of us has a special purpose and meaning.

For example, one day a woman told me that she wanted to open her own boutique, and she wanted to ask me a few questions about getting started. She said it had been her dream since she was a little girl. She was now forty-eight, her kids were grown and in college, and time was no longer an excuse. I listened to her story, and it was like so many others I've heard: excuse after excuse—not enough time, not enough money, not enough connections.

I have heard this story so many times that I was just frustrated. So when this woman finished, I simply said, "What if you could do it? What if it became the most successful boutique in the area? What if you won awards? What if you could impact the community in ways you never imagined?" I kept going for a minute, and the woman's eyes got bigger and bigger. She was clearly thinking, "I never thought of it that way before." We are programmed to look at the "everything that could go wrong" side of our dreams, and we're told that to look at the "everything could go right" scenario is naïve and childish. Maybe too idealistic. I beg to differ.

In my journey, my greatest asset has been my ability to rethink my fears and doubts by asking two huge questions:

"What if?"
"Why not?"

"What if?" and "Why not?" are the most powerful questions in my universe. They empower me by reminding me to embrace the "everything could go right" scenario and to imagine all the great possibilities. I wasn't born with this positive attitude. For years, my

6

greatest fear was letting people down or facing ridicule. I was the kid who would often withdraw from situations or activities in case I failed, because I was uncomfortable with being laughed at or disappointing others.

People who meet me today can't believe this was the case. They say things like, "I'll bet everything has always been easy for you." This makes me laugh, because the opposite is so true. But years ago, I taught myself to reframe those questions that make us all fear failure and doubt our own abilities. I started to ask myself, "What if I didn't worry about what other people thought of my failures?" Today, when I find myself faced with a fear like, "People will think my idea is crazy," I have trained myself to instantly ask, "What if my crazy ideas inspire and positively impact other people to help me bring them to life?" or, "Why not share them so I can find others who are as inspired by them as I am?" When you start asking these kinds of "What if?" and "Why not?" questions, you rethink your fears. You turn them into potential and then into reality. Today, when someone says, "Jen, that's crazy," I think, "Fantastic! I must be on to something!" Original thinking is *always* ridiculed until it becomes accepted wisdom.

Try it now. If you've been feeling intimidated by the idea of all the hard work that goes into starting your own business, ask yourself, "What if working hard and having fun were the same thing?" That's the wonderful secret of entrepreneurship that no one tells you but you need to know. When you're doing something you love, even if you're working longer hours than ever, you'll never get tired. If you think of it that way, doesn't the hard work seem incidental to loving what you're doing every day of your life? It does for me.

I remember when I developed my habit of asking these questions into a strategic tool. When I was launching the Butler Bag Company, everyone in the industry told me that my concept wouldn't work. The first few times I sat in meetings and heard the doubts, I became defensive. That only prompted others to defend their points of view, which got us nowhere. One day, I was sitting in yet another meeting with people questioning my ideas and telling me what I couldn't do. Finally, I realized that I needed to stop defending myself. Instead, I asked, "What if my idea does work? What if it redefines the industry and you had a chance to be a part of it and chose not to?" The change was stunning. The person sitting across the table from me was no longer defensive. He stopped and gave serious thought to what I had said. The power was all flowing toward me, allowing new perspectives to emerge. This changed everything.

What Do You Fear More, Failure or Regret?

Years ago, I had several product ideas that I didn't launch because I was afraid of failure. I saw some of them come to market in the hands of other people. One day, I was sitting in a rocking chair on my front porch (I know, an ironic image) and I thought, "You know, regret is much worse than failure." That idea set me free to take risks and stop worrying about falling on my face. When you try to bring your idea to life, even if it falls short, you'll always be proud that you tried, and you'll learn tremendous lessons from the experience.

People fear failure because they see failure as a verdict about their abilities. But when fear stops you from acting on your ideas and dreams, you're selling your legacy short. You're guaranteeing yourself a lifetime of regrets. Do you want to be sitting around at the end of your life saying, "I wish I had . . ."? Or would you rather be talking about the risks you took, the spectacular failures you experienced, the turnarounds you engineered, the things you created, and the lives you changed? You will never regret the leaps of faith or the big mistakes; you will only regret the things you don't try and the dreams you don't pursue. The fear of regret can be motivating and inspiring.

Failure is misunderstood in our culture. I was speaking at a leadership conference, and a young man stood up and said, "You're telling us about the entrepreneurs who have succeeded, but what about the ones who failed? Why don't you tell us about them?" I smiled. Talk about a perfect setup. I said, "I have told you about the ones who have failed, because all these successful ones failed many, many times. They just didn't let that stop them from getting back up and trying again." Failure is the fuel for success; entrepreneurs understand this. I'm always creating, pushing the envelope, and taking a new risk. If one idea fails, so what? I've got more. So do you.

In this book I share with you the fears I encounter most often in people who are passionate about living their dreams and starting their own businesses. As you will learn through my stories, your fears were once my fears (and they still are from time to time). However, shifting your perspective can set you free and take away your fear of failure so you can start your business and achieve your goals. Most entrepreneurs don't know exactly how to get from A to Z when they start, but they have the belief that somehow they will get there. So will you.

Entrepreneurship Is Self-Transformation

The most important thing you can take away from *What If? & Why Not?* is this: **Entrepreneurship is not about business. It is about self-transformation.** It is about becoming who you have always wanted to be. It is a 180-degree shift in perspective and mind-set—then living every day with that mind-set. You stare at yourself every day, see your weaknesses close up, and find new ways to overcome them. If you're approaching entrepreneurship correctly, it is transformative. As an entrepreneur, you should be in a constant state of personal growth. Launching yourself out into space with nothing but a wing, a prayer, an idea, and a business plan, far outside your comfort bubble, will change who you are and how you live more completely than any self-help program, religious conversion, or psychotherapy.

One day, I would love to poll entrepreneurs who fall into two groups: the wildly successful and the ones who gave up after a short while. I'll bet you that 90 percent of the wildly successful ones spent more time working on themselves than their companies, because they knew that they *are* their companies. They have cultivated their passion, their self-belief, and their ability to inspire others every day. They spend less time working on balance sheets and fine-tuning marketing plans and more time finding new ways to overcome their fears and bring audacious new ideas to light. **That's what entrepreneurs do: they change the world by changing themselves first.**

Ideas aren't just about product development or financial success; they are part of your identity. You show the world who you are through the expression and development of your ideas. When I talk to aspiring entrepreneurs who never got their idea off the drawing board, I hear the same sad story: it's not the idea they don't believe in, but their own ability to make it work. They don't believe they have what it takes to be a Tommy Hilfiger or a Jeff Bezos or a Mark Zuckerberg, the college kid who created Facebook. But do you know the only quality separating those moguls from other people? Self-belief and the willingness to shove the fear back in the corners of their minds and trust their ideas. The fire to go for it and let the chips fall where they may.

The first question to ask yourself when you think about taking the entrepreneurial leap isn't, "What kind of business do I want to start?" It's, "Who do I want to become?" The first thing you must change before you can realize your dream is yourself. Call it the spiritual path to entrepreneurship if you like, but ask anyone who has built something great from nothing and he or she will back me up. When you start there, everything else falls into place.

Hit the Mental Reset Button

You know the feeling you get when you have a marvelous idea that you know could change your life and maybe the world? You can't sleep, your mind races, and you fill pages of yellow pads with sketches, product names, and business plans. You're more fired up than you've been in years until you hit that fear or doubt about money, management, or something else that drains all that giddy energy away. You sigh, say, "I guess it wasn't meant to be," and put the pad in a drawer. The lights go out on that dream.

There are no statistics on businesses that never get started because of that sort of fear, but I'll bet millions of potentially successful companies stop before they start each year because entrepreneurs lose their nerve. But what if you could get past that point? What if you could develop tools that would get you beyond dreaming into actually doing? You would be 90 percent of the way to opening your doors. The rest—business plans, accounting, manufacturing, hiring, and so on—is just procedure. If you have passion and desire and the will to act on them, you have almost everything you need to make your idea a reality and launch your company—to become your own boss, which is what this is all about.

In *What If? & Why Not?* I help you make the critical mental paradigm shift that you need to get past that fear- and doubt-based stopping point to start and sustain the company you've been dreaming and scheming about. I help you learn to rethink your fears and doubts in the moment they arise, as if you're pushing an instant mental reset button. I'm at a point where, when a negative thought enters my mind, I can hit my mental reset button and bring in a positive thought instead. In this book, I share with you the secrets to doing that.

I talk a great deal about *branding* and why your brand is the most important asset your new business has. The Butler Bag is a brand. Jen Groover is a brand. A brand is a promise to your customer—a promise that carries tremendous emotional power. If you can build and grow a brand that your customers love and are happy to tell other people about, you stand a great chance of being successful. In this book, I share with you some of the best ways I've learned to make that happen.

I help you ask empowering new questions that reverse fears and doubts, and take immediate productive action. This is a mind-set of longevity—of not just starting a business but keeping it going and growing it into whatever you're dreaming of. First, I show you how, by asking yourself positive, affirming "What if?" questions, you can erase doubts and fears and realize how much you can do with your ideas. Second, I suggest "Why not?" questions and practical steps you can take right now to deal with everything from finances and legal protection to marketing and your fears of failure.

I ask you to take immediate action, and by that I mean as soon as you set down this book. At the end of each chapter, I give you a to-do list of things you can do in the next twenty-four hours that will move you closer to starting your business. I know that's demanding, but nothing gets you past fears and doubts better than taking instant action and seeing that "Yes, I really can do this!"

I also invite you to write your "Dream Plan" as we go through this journey together. This isn't a business plan; those are about executive summaries and financials. The Dream Plan is about your life and your vision. Remember that this is more about who you want to become than the technical side of your business. In each chapter, you'll fill in one more part of the Dream Plan so that by the end of the book, you'll have a complete blueprint for success. Then, send it to me at whatifandwhynot.com. I'll be taking a look at them. I might even give you a call to talk about it. Who knows? Maybe we could end up in business together!

A quick note: The parts of the Dream Plan don't always coincide with the content of the chapters. The Dream Plan is a step-by-step business plan development tool that covers some areas that this book doesn't cover. But both the book and your Dream Plan will complement each other, and what you learn in each chapter will help you make your plan the best it can be.

This book is not is a guide to following Jen's dream. I don't want you to follow my path; I want you to create your own. You don't have to be Bill Gates or Martha Stewart and create multimillion-dollar companies to be a successful, thrilled, ecstatically happy entrepreneur. **Entrepreneurship is about creating a lifestyle that you love.** It could mean becoming a freelance consultant or publicist, starting your own ad-supported blog, or opening a retail store to sell your handicrafts. Your first goal should be to make a good living doing something you absolutely adore. Beyond that—well, you'll know the opportunities when you see them.

There are four vital assets to starting a business:

- Desire
- Passion
- A great idea
- Absolute belief in yourself

I know you have all four. All you need is to put them into motion. This book is my promise to you that if you learn to get past your fears and doubts and believe in yourself and your vision, and dedicate yourself to hard work and perseverance, you can and will succeed. This is about self-actualization and self-fulfillment— becoming the person you've always known you could be and living the life you've always known you deserved. You deserve to love your life and not just live for the weekends. When you love what you're doing and take risks to create something you're passionate about, you'll never work a day in your life. I work very hard, but I never feel like I need a vacation. Millions of others are just as fortunate. There is no reason you can't be, too.

"What if I have a great idea but don't know how to turn it into a business?"

Welcome to the age of the entrepreneur as superhero. The story of the rogue entrepreneur has become 100 percent Hollywood cliché. It goes like this: Young, brilliant rebel enters college, gets bored, stays up for forty-eight hours at a time in his dorm inventing something crazy cool, and his invention takes the campus and then the country by storm. Then he shocks his family and friends by quitting college, starting his own company, and becoming a billionaire at an age when most people are just starting to pay down their student loans.

Only happens in movies, right? Nope. It happened not that long ago to a kid named Mark Zuckerberg. You don't know him, you say. Well, maybe you know what he created while he was a student at Harvard: Facebook. Chances are you're on it. I certainly am. It's one of my most important branding and communication tools. And in early 2009, this former social network for college students passed the 200-million-user mark. Zuckerberg himself, now only twenty-five and still looking like the grinning, slightly geeky guy who delivered your pizza last Saturday, has a net worth estimated

15

by *Forbes* to be about $1.5 billion. He even had the guts to turn down an offer from Yahoo to buy the site in 2006—*for a billion dollars*. That's the kind of offer that young tech wizards whisper about late at night when they warm their hands around their flat-panel computer screens.

Zuckerberg not only trusted his idea and vision enough to launch Facebook, but also to turn down massive money so that he could maintain control over his creation. He did this because it's not just about starting the company, but seeing the company through its growth, staying true to the vision. He could not have known right away what it would become—he intended it strictly as a network for college kids, and only over time did it blossom into a global connection tool for people of all ages—but he knew that it would become something worthwhile.

Ideas Are Cheap, but Great Ideas Are Priceless

If I had a nickel for every time someone told me, "I had an idea, but I just didn't know what to do with it," I could hang up my Butler Bag and retire to Bermuda. I hear this sort of thing all the time from people, and what's sad is that, years after getting excited down to their bones about an idea, they are still hanging on to it without having ever done a single thing to make it reality. What I can't bear to tell them is that if they haven't already acted on their idea, odds are that someone else has—and turned it into a business. I know. I've been there.

Do you really think the company that's marketing the Snuggie (the blanket with sleeves!) was launched by the first person to have that idea? Of course not. All it takes to come up with the Snuggie is to accidentally put your robe on backwards and have a light come on over your head. But it takes a certain kind of mind to see the inspiration in everyday situations. Ninety-nine percent of people who might put their robe on backwards would just smack themselves in the head and put the thing on the other way, never giving it another thought.

A person with an entrepreneur's mind puts that robe on the wrong way and thinks, "Wait a second. What if this was the right way?" I don't think for a second that I was the first woman to be exasperated with my handbag and look for a better way to organize it. But as far as I know, I was the first to find inspiration in my dishwasher rack, see the potential for a business, and make that idea a reality. Having an idea is wonderful; ideas transform the world. But unless you can turn ideas into physical reality, they are just interesting mental exercises.

The company making millions off the Snuggie is the one where someone said, "I can make this idea into a best-selling product" and ran with the ball. Now there are would-be entrepreneurs all over the internet claiming that the people behind the Snuggie stole their idea and threatening lawsuits. That seems to me like sour grapes, because someone else had an inspiration, saw its potential, and had the courage and self-belief to take a risk. Always remember it's not enough to have a great idea. You must also have great execution to turn your idea into a thriving business.

You're reading this book, so I already know that you have an entrepreneur's mind. Maybe all you're looking for is something to move you to the next step—to help you find the courage to take the risk that others can't take. With that in mind, let's talk about the biggest obstacle facing any entrepreneur.

Fear Factor Isn't Just an Old Reality Show

Lack of knowledge is not the real reason that most people spend more time regretting than doing. It's an excuse. Thanks to Facebook, LinkedIn, blogs, and Google, if you want to find someone to share the nuts and bolts of raising capital, applying for a patent, or designing a logo, you can do it in minutes. When you really believe in your vision, you will find a way to acquire the knowledge you need. But that's just the technical know-how. The real reason most people don't get out of the starting gate with their ideas is fear, and overcoming fear is something you have to do for yourself. Again, entrepreneurship is all about personal development.

Ideas are extensions of who we are; when I launch a new product, I'm sending a piece of myself out into the world and hoping that others will embrace it. That's risky and scary, but that's what being an entrepreneur is about. In a way, it's like being an actor. You're always standing on that chorus line, auditioning for the director, hoping this time to get the part. That's the reality, and if you can't get past the fear of scrutiny, you become a "wantrepreneur," someone who talks about starting a business but never gets around to it.

The idea of starting a company can be overwhelming. There's a huge amount of work to be done. There's nothing easy about taking a product idea, a concept for a book, a speaking platform, or a new business model for running restaurants and turning it into a way to make a living. Many people are stopped dead by the fear that, with so much to learn and do, they're not up to the challenge. They are paralyzed by fears that are either unlikely or not anywhere near as bad as they think. These are the five most common fears I see in the frustrated would-be moguls I meet:

1. *Fear of not being good enough.* They think they have to learn everything about starting a business on their own and manage the entire show themselves, and some nagging voice inside says, "You don't have what it takes." They probably do, but if they don't try, they'll never know.
2. *Fear of ridicule.* They fear being made fun of and friends and family thinking they've gone off the deep end. But everyone who chases a dream is accused of having lost it at one point or another. If they all listened, we'd go nowhere.

18

3. *Fear of poverty.* There is no rule that says you have to spend a fortune to launch a business or quit your job right away to do it. Most businesses are started in the entrepreneur's spare time with money from savings, friends, and family.

4. *Fear of being consumed.* They fear that the business will take all their time and leave them with none for family, hobbies, and leisure. It can. I have seen people become consumed with their companies. But it doesn't have to be that way if you remember that any business is only a means to two ends: being the person you have always wanted to be and living the life that you have always wanted to live. If you keep those priorities in front of you, you will grow your business in a way that provides balance. Remember that it's not work when you love what you do; it's more like leisure time.

5. *Fear of change.* Your life has to change if you're going to start a business! But entrepreneurship is the most powerful force for positive change in the world. If you're passionate about something and you have the opportunity to make it the center of your daily life, that's a change worth making.

If you're passionate enough about your idea and you can get past these fears, you will find ways to get the knowledge you need to make your idea happen.

Lone Entrepreneur Syndrome

When you were a kid and you didn't know what to do in a situation, what did you do? You asked someone who knew—usually a grown-up or maybe an older sibling. Well, life doesn't change very much in that regard. People are still going to be your best resource for business knowledge. One of the most valuable lessons I have learned is this:

People like to share what they know.

"Lone entrepreneur syndrome" kills a lot of companies in their infancy. In the beginning, people don't have a budget to hire a website developer, so they try to do it themselves. They don't have the money for a bookkeeper, so they try to do it themselves. Those are major tactical mistakes. You're the visionary. If you're jumping from creative tasks and visioning to daily operation tasks like accounting and shipping, you're not leveraging yourself in the best way. No one has the ability to do everything needed to run a company. If you don't know how to get started, ask someone who has built a company from scratch. If you don't know about leasing office space, talk to a business owner. If you don't know about financials, talk to an accountant, bookkeeper, or controller. If you're clueless about marketing, ask friends how they developed their marketing strategies or talk to someone who develops them for a living. People love to share their experiences. Just make sure to show gratitude when they do.

How to Find Great Partners

One of the most important first steps you can take is to build the team of people who will help you get your idea off the ground. Bring in people you can trust to become partners. A lot of new entrepreneurs are gun-shy about partnerships because they've heard horror stories. The wrong partners can create toxic personal chemistry, spark power struggles, or waste scarce capital. You should always select your partners with great care. But finding the *right* partners can bring invaluable complementary skills and knowledge to your company and give you a big competitive advantage.

For example, my partner in the Butler Bag Company and Jen Groover Productions is the detail guy. He's the skeptic. He's the one who analyzes and questions everything. I'm the one going on my faith in human beings and basing my decisions on a handshake and what people say. I can't help it; I'm a passionate person. I'm the one who says, "Yeah, let's do it!" He says, "Wait a minute." He grounds me. He's the perfect counterpart to my "leap before you look" approach, because he's cautious and asks great, probing questions.

Partnering or teaming with others should be about knowing your strong points and finding your opposite, the yang to your yin. When you are writing down your initial thoughts and plans for your business, it's very helpful to create a list labeled "Things that could prevent me from succeeding." Then write down all the possible land mines that could blow up your business before it really gets going. Many of them will involve lack of knowledge or personality traits that could be detrimental if they're not balanced out. For instance, I don't like details or confrontation. My partner handles both beautifully. So those two qualities, which could hurt my company if I was by myself, are counterbalanced.

The following is my advice on selecting partners when you're starting your company.

1. *List the assets that your company needs.* For instance, if you're not great with technology and your company will depend on the internet, consider a partner who knows the Net. If you have great ideas but no idea about things like business licenses, contracts, trademarks, and regulation, perhaps you should consider finding a partner with a legal background.

2. *Recruit a genius with numbers.* If you're not a numbers person (I'm not, and many visionaries are not), make sure you have a partner who is. Numbers are the lifeblood of any business. You must have someone who can keep the books, who understands profits and expenses, and who runs a tight financial ship. Your money person should be so on top of the finances that you're almost uncomfortable about it. Your company will fall apart without this.

3. *Remember that you're not getting married.* Just because you are working with one partner on one project doesn't mean that

person has to be part of everything else you do for the rest of your life. You may want to structure the deal in a way that gives both of you an "out clause" if neither partner is happy, or work on a project-by-project basis.

4. *Give partners "skin in the game."* Meaning give them a share of ownership in the company, but base its value on the company's performance. Partners might come to you with money to invest, but I believe in giving partners part of the company so they are more motivated to help build something that will reward them financially. At the outset, if you have a truly inspiring business idea, a piece of ownership of that idea is the best (and often the only) carrot you have to dangle in front of people.

5. *Trust your instincts.* You should always vet potential partners (you can do background checks, but personal references and Googling names should be enough), but *you should also trust your gut.* If a potential partner says or does things that make you feel he or she isn't right, despite a great résumé, walk away.

6. *Be prepared to surrender some control.* If you're going to give people part of your company in return for their sweat, you won't get to have things 100 percent your way anymore. If you have a "this is MY idea, and it has to be MY way!" mentality, you're going to be a lone entrepreneur again before too long. If you go to the trouble of finding smart, talented people who complement your weaknesses, you'll do well to listen to them. The right-brained and left-brained need each other. A lot of companies die because of a lack of collaboration.

The best way to find partners, hands down, is to network. There is a spiritual side to my business, and it revolves around the belief that if I go out there with the right intention, I will find the person I need. You've heard the saying "When the student is ready, the teacher appears"? Well, when the entrepreneur is ready, the partners will appear. That has happened to me again and again.

Don't make the mistake of holing up in an office doing busy-work when you should be out meeting people and networking. Even with the internet, there is no substitute for going out and shaking hands. I love Twitter, Facebook, and LinkedIn; they are fantastic "distance networking" tools. I highly recommend that you be on all three and be active. But you simply must be out meeting people and shaking hands at industry events, fund-raisers, trade shows, and the like. Nothing compares to the face-to-face human connection. If you do that in the spirit of seeking and discovery, partners will find you.

Dreamer's Corner: A New Entrepreneur Q&A

Eric Leebow, Founder
www.freezecrowd.com
eric.leebow@gmail.com

1. What is the name of your new business, and when did you start it?

FreezeCrowd, Inc. launched freezecrowd.com in 2009. However, I came up with beginnings of the idea as early as 1999 with a dream idea that I had by looking at my college freshman "meet me" book from Lehigh University. It's something I held inside my mind for a while and came up with some very interesting, yet possibly executable ideas. I think we all start businesses in our minds, but it's those who put their minds to work, share their ideas with others, and put their ideas to action who actually start.

2. What type of business is it?

FreezeCrowd is an interactive social networking site for college students and alumni. We are unique because we connect people in interesting ways through the group photos and provide an interactive and informational experience for the end user.

(continued)

3. What was the greatest obstacle you faced in starting your business, and how did you overcome it?

Hiring good people and finding the right people the first time around. I hired and trusted way too many people, and although some let me down, I still followed through with my dreams, because I knew that just because you don't find the right people the first time around, doesn't mean your idea or vision isn't unique. One thing I have is tenacity; all entrepreneurs need to be tenacious. In business, there is no such thing as a business failing; it's only successful people who have moved on to something else. Although this is not the first business I've started, I know that if you keep following through with something you're passionate about, or really like the idea of, it will succeed.

4. What has the experience of being an entrepreneur taught you about yourself, and how has it changed you?

I believe that coming up with a great idea is one thing. It's another to actually make it happen. I do not believe being an entrepreneur has changed me; it has just made me think a little more deeply about things that most people do not think about doing. If anything, it helped me realize that one person's great idea can have an impact on others.

5. What is the most important lesson you have learned about starting a business?

You can't do everything by yourself, but you must find people who are smarter than you to work with you. You must find good people the first time. Not everyone in the world believes in your dreams as passionately as you do, and you aren't always the most skilled person to fulfill the dream yourself. You need to connect with people who believe in your vision.

6. Where is your business today as far as earnings, size, etc.? What are your prospects for the future?

Currently we are a start-up and a private company. Our prospect for the future is to expand our market and reach out to the masses. We aspire to make FreezeCrowd the most innovative social networking phenomenon ever, connecting people in group photos and enabling them to break the ice in crowds everywhere. FreezeCrowd will change the world and make a difference in the lives of many!

"What If?" and "Why Not?" Questions

Welcome to my first set of questions designed to help you rethink your fears and doubts. The chapter titles are the most common negative questions I hear when I speak with new entrepreneurs— their greatest fears. I've responded with two types of questions. The "What if?" questions are intended to reverse fearful thinking by asking, basically, "What if things go well?"

The "Why not?" questions are about opening your mind to paths forward that you may not have considered. They represent ideas, strategies, and bold moves toward problem solving— exactly the kinds of steps that every successful entrepreneur needs to take.

A lot of the heavy lifting in becoming a successful entrepreneur involves not so much working on your company as yourself. If you can shift your perspective away from negative thinking and clear away mental and emotional obstacles, then the financial, organizational, manufacturing, and marketing parts are comparatively simple.

What if starting a business is not as complicated as you think?

Business doesn't always have to be complex at the outset, especially if you're launching a service company. My focus tends to be on products since I'm in the business of creating brands around tangible items, but there are a hundred other ways to set out on your own that are much simpler. If your goal is to become a self-employed bookkeeper, writer, or graphic designer, then all you need is an office space, a computer, a phone, a website, and maybe a few specific tools. In general, I have found that the simpler you can keep things at the outset, the better. You're going to have a learning curve. You're going to feel nervous and excited. Having fewer moving parts means fewer decisions to make, and that lets you get your feet wet at a pace that you're comfortable with.

I've made a couple of TV appearances in which I talk about how to start a business on less than $50. You can still find them on YouTube, but here are the basic tools and resources you'll need to have in place:

- *Company name.*
    * WHAT: You should register your company name with your county clerk's office as a sole proprietorship. Later on when you start to grow, you can consult an attorney about creating an LLC or a corporation.
    * WHY: You need legal ownership of your name to get a business license or incorporate.
    * HOW MUCH: The fee varies according to your county.
- *Business cards.*
    * WHAT: Business cards are a primary branding piece.
    * WHY: They are important because they're something to hand to every new contact that carries your contact information and also builds your brand.
    * HOW MUCH: You can get hundreds of business cards for as little as $9.99 at a site like 123print.com or VistaPrint.com.
- *Website.*
    * WHAT: Your website is your online branding center, brochure, communications hub, and storefront.
    * WHY: Customers, vendors, potential partners, and the media will use the Web as their primary source of information about your company. It needs to be clean, easy to use, informative, and most importantly, functioning.
    * HOW MUCH: You can launch your website by purchasing a domain name at a site like GoDaddy.com for about $9.99 a year. Many domain registry sites also have excellent web-

site builder tools that will let you create your site in a few hours even if you lack programming skills.

- *Bank account.*
  * **WHAT:** This is a dedicated business checking account.
  * **WHY:** You need a separate business account for legal and accounting reasons—to keep your personal finances separate from company books. This also helps you establish a relationship with a business bank, which can come in handy later if you are looking for a loan or credit line.
  * **HOW MUCH:** Find a bank that works well with small business owners, has later hours, and has services to manage your cash flow. Setting up the account should cost nothing.
- *Social networking.*
  * **WHAT:** You should have active pages on Facebook and Twitter, the two most popular social networking websites.
  * **WHY:** This is crucial because hundreds of millions of Web users find businesses, tell their friends about them, and track their activities via these sites.
  * **HOW MUCH:** You can be out there instantly on Facebook and Twitter, and it's 100 percent free. It takes about fifteen minutes to get your pages up and running.
- *Business license.*
  * **WHAT:** A business license is a document from the local jurisdiction that handles business affairs that says you are legally permitted to be in business and also registers you as a business for tax purposes.
  * **WHY:** You may not need one; it depends on your local government. You will need a license if you want to open a retail store or provide a professional service that's regulated by the government.
  * **HOW MUCH:** This will vary. Visit businesslicenses.com, a fantastic website where you can learn if you need a license and order it if you do.

- *Office space.*
  - * **WHAT:** Office space is dedicated space in which to engage in activities that are solely about your business.
  - * **WHY:** You will be much more productive if you have a business-only workplace that minimizes distractions.
  - * **HOW MUCH:** Office space can be very expensive. If you don't need it, don't lease it. Instead, consider an "executive suite," one of those shared office hives where you get an office, use of shared conference facilities, and a receptionist for a lower fee. But if you can work from home at first, do it, because you're already paying for the space.
- *Personnel.*
  - * **WHAT:** Don't hire anyone right away if you can avoid it.
  - * **WHY:** Hiring means paying payroll taxes and workers' compensation, as well as complying with a raft of laws. At the outset, bring people in as interns or "sweat equity" partners (people who earn ownership shares in exchange for their work), or hire people as independent contractors.
  - * **HOW MUCH:** You'll save a fortune in salaries, taxes, and benefits by sticking with contractors (who get paid a fee only) and sweat equity partners.
- *Legal services.*
  - * **WHAT:** You will need legal advice if your business involves contracts, trademarks, patents, compliance with local laws, or a variety of other issues.
  - * **WHY:** Not having at least some basic legal groundwork laid can cost you money, invite litigation, and even put you out of business.
  - * **HOW MUCH:** Websites like LegalZoom.com can be a godsend for simple legal activities like trademark and patent filings. You can file a simple trademark via the site for $494, nearly $1,000 less than a typical attorney's fee. If you need a lawyer, ask for referrals or try FindLaw.com.

- *Financials.*
  * **WHAT:** You need a controller, bookkeeper, or accountant with business financial experience. When you're starting out, a bookkeeper is probably sufficient.
  * **WHY:** Financial order is everything for a new business. You need to know how much money is going out and coming in down to the penny.
  * **HOW MUCH:** A simple way to get off on the right foot with bookkeeping and taxes is to use a company like Accountemps (accountemps.com), which hires out accountants on a project or temporary basis. Costs vary, but because you're not paying benefits or payroll taxes, you'll save money.

Starting a manufacturing company or a brick-and-mortar store can cost a lot more, so work up to that slowly. Establish yourself first. Don't panic. I know that list looks like a lot to deal with. But we'll be going over many of these steps again, and they will become less intimidating. Remember, you're going to start simply: you, a great idea, a computer, and some business cards. You can add the rest of the list as you go. Go step by step and you'll be amazed at how much easier it becomes to lay the groundwork for your company.

Why not write a business plan to help to manage the start-up details?

A business plan is a document that lays out all the details involved in your company: what it makes or sells, who its customers are, how it makes money, who operates it, and so on. Conventional entrepreneurial wisdom considers a formal business plan a must-have for every new business. However, you'll notice that I left it off my list above. The reason is simple: I don't think a business plan is always necessary when you're starting out. Certainly at some point in your business life, you will need one if you are going to seek funding or run a larger organization. But if you are planning on being a solo practitioner for life or running a small, self-funded operation then you don't always need a formal business plan.

The danger in focusing on your business plan is that it can become a surrogate for actually starting your business. You spend years perfecting the business plan, and it becomes a great delaying tactic for starting your company. "I can't start my business yet; I'm still working on my business plan," is a common refrain. Most of those business plans will never see the light of day. Many successful entrepreneurs did not have a formal, written business plan when they started out, but they had a great plan in their head (and a clear vision) to tell them where they should be going next.

However, if you find yourself paralyzed by everything you have to do to get your company off the ground, a simple business plan can be a fantastic tool to help you make sense of things and set priorities. Here's what I recommend you include in a simplified business blueprint:

- The name of your business, a tagline, and a mission statement
- Your core product or service
- How you will fund the business and what it will cost
- Who your market is
- What your pricing will be
- How you will market and build your brand (how you will stand out and be different)
- How you will operate (from your house, from an office, etc.)
- How you will produce your product
- How and where you will sell your product or service
- What your website will include
- Possible allies, mentors, and customers that you know about today
- The action items you need to complete to get started within sixty days

Keep it simple. Don't start adding financials, executive summaries, and all that; that's usually where people panic and get stuck. You'll also notice that this plan has a built-in deadline of sixty days. That's because I want you to create your plan, refine it, and have your business up and running in two months. That way you don't get so caught up in writing your plan that you lose the fire to launch your company.

If you find yourself stuck, here are some online resources that will give you sample business plans, tips on writing a better plan, and even video guides:

- sba.gov/smallbusinessplanner/plan/writeabusinessplan/index.html
- bplans.com
- businessplans.org/index.asp
- myownbusiness.org

What if experienced people will be eager to help you?

As I said, people love to share what they know. So rather than feel like you're all alone in a harsh business world that's waiting to trip you up, realize that you're actually part of a community of entrepreneurs. Some of those entrepreneurs have become amazingly successful and love helping people who are where they used to be. I think that's universal to human nature: we recognize people who are on the same journey as we are, and because the journey has been so rewarding for us, we want to help others have the same experience. That's why I mentor new entrepreneurs, and it's why you will have no trouble locating experienced people to advise you on everything from manufacturing and legal services to marketing and hiring.

Some people have taken this idea to the next level and created organized small business mentoring programs. One of the best is the Small Business Mentoring Project in British Columbia, Canada (smallbusinessmentor.bc.ca). The network pairs registered mentors and "protégés" who work in the same communities, so they can meet face-to-face and discuss business challenges. I also love the Service Corps of Retired Executives (SCORE) Association. It's a nonprofit association that is dedicated to entrepreneur education and the success of small business nationwide. There are 389 SCORE chapters around the United States. You can find a chapter near you at score.org.

I've had very good experiences with people sharing their business lessons and warnings with me. However, *be serious when you ask someone for help.* I can definitely say it turns me off when I can tell that a person who asks for my advice clearly isn't serious. When you're not serious, you're wasting the time of someone who is busy and successful and probably doesn't have time to waste. If you're serious about seeking help, you'll *know what you want to learn from someone*, and you'll be clear about what you are trying to achieve with your questions. I love questions like "I notice that you are growing your brand through various licensing deals. How did you do that? What was your inspiration?" That tells me the questioner has taken the time to learn about me and my company, so he or she is probably serious about using whatever advice I can offer. Prepare a few specific questions in advance of a meeting with a formal mentor or attending a networking event.

You can get an incredible business education through formal mentoring (which I talk more about later in the book) or by just talking with experienced, successful people over cocktails or at a trade show. But a mentor or model doesn't have to be someone with whom you have a personal relationship. It can be someone you follow whose actions inspire you. Apple CEO Steve Jobs is a personal hero for me because of his daring, incredibly creative strategic decisions. I've never met the man (yet), but I've learned a lot from him.

Why not · · · start your own mastermind group?

If you start with the "who," the "what" will take care of itself. Finding the right people to advise you is everything. I wish I could whisper this into the ear of every fledgling entrepreneur and small business owner: "Start your own mastermind group."

A mastermind group is a group of motivated, like-minded individuals who unite to form a brain trust and work together toward the goals of all the members. Mastermind groups come in all different shapes, forms, and sizes (i.e., a group of golfing buddies, a Tuesday lunch or cocktail group, a group that meets and communicates internationally via the Web), and there are no set rules for how they form, operate, or govern or how long they exist. The only requirement is that there is a dynamic of trust, respect, admiration, positivity, support, commitment, and fun. The five best reasons to start your own group are:

1. *Creative enhancement.* Ideas need collective input from different perspectives to develop. When a group is able to brainstorm and meditate together on one idea, that idea has no choice but to grow. Even if your idea, at the end, remains unchanged, you will have new confidence knowing that it has been thoroughly vetted. Brainstorming with others also creates a breeding ground for new ideas.
2. *Networking and building business relationships.* Sharing your goals with others exposes your needs. Often these needs will involve enlisting outside help, and members of your mastermind group may be your gateway to people you need to meet. Each member's contacts should ultimately become the group's contacts, and any introduction that is made on behalf of a fellow group member should be made with complete

confidence or not at all. Business relationships are built on credibility and trust, and when outside people and businesses are thrilled to get a referral from within your group, the group becomes more powerful.

3. *Resource enhancement.* Although members of your group should be somewhat like-minded, it also helps if each brings unique knowledge or resources to the table. For example, a member who needs certain printed materials may find that one member has free access to printing equipment and another has the production background to run the job properly. Such collaborative resources can save you untold amounts of time and money.

4. *Accountability.* We are more likely to stick to something when others have a vested interest in our involvement. It's always more difficult to let others down. When you make a commitment and state your goals to the group, you are making yourself responsible for taking action and seeing those goals through.

5. *Motivation.* Everyone has good days and bad days, but when you enter the world of entrepreneurial business, those highs and lows increase exponentially. Having business friends to lean on in these moments of doubt is critical to ensuring that you jump back on the horse the moment you fall off.

As T. Harv Eker says, "Your network is your net worth." Entrepreneurs have a tendency to try to tackle everything themselves. Mastermind groups provide camaraderie and productivity while giving you access to people who have been where you are trying to go. To find or create one, try Meetup.com. There are hundreds of business roundtables and brainstorming groups meeting around the country already!

What if you already have the qualities you need to start your company?

Inexperienced entrepreneurs tend to focus on the nuts and bolts of starting a company, from hiring practices to raising capital. But those things are not going to make your company a success. It's very likely, in fact, that you already have what you need to make your company a winner: your passion, vision, and commitment.

Remember that a business is nothing less than a reflection of you. The company's development will follow the same arc as your personal growth. No matter how smoothly your accounting office might run or how slick and powerful your branding is, it won't make a difference if you're not in love with what you're doing; feel a sense of ironclad commitment to your customers; and have a bold, creative vision that you stick to no matter how many people tell you it's impossible.

You can learn the skills you need to operate a business, from making marketing budgets to writing a business plan, but you can't learn the "character equity" that makes any business fly. You either have the burning desire to make your dream a reality and a creative vision that won't let you sleep at night, or you don't. If you have those things, my advice to you is to quit worrying about the mechanics of business that you don't know and get moving. Create forward motion. Start your company, even if it's just you at your dining room table. The rest will take care of itself.

Why not jump out of the plane?

If you know you have the passion, desire, and commitment, why not just do it? Jumping out of the plane means quitting your job or doing something else that gives you no choice but to either start your business or go bankrupt. It pushes you past the point of no return. That may seem drastic, and for some people who have a lot of debt or other financial challenges, it may not be an option. I understand that. But many of us take action only when the situation gives us no other choice, and if you have been dithering around for years with your business idea without ever moving on it, and you're still saying, "Someday," then you may have to face the fact that you will never chase your dream unless you put yourself in a position in which you have no other option.

This takes guts and a lot of honesty, but it's a fantastic way to motivate yourself to learn business skills and start your company now after what might be years of procrastinating. I'm not suggesting that you walk out on your job tomorrow; you shouldn't commit fiscal suicide or breach a contract. But giving thirty days' notice or hiring someone can be very motivating and can give you a little time to get your financial affairs in order. (See Chapter 3 for more on the minimum savings you should have before taking the plunge.) Here are the keys to a successful jump:

- *Use the time window to save capital.* You probably won't get a severance package if you resign, but it doesn't hurt to ask. Can you cash in unused vacation time? Get every cent you can to use toward your company.
- *Start making sales.* Don't wait until you actually leave your job to start generating revenue. There's nothing stopping you from selling right now.
- *Network like a maniac.* Launch your Facebook, Twitter, and LinkedIn accounts right away, and start leveraging them. Go to Meetup.com and look for small business owner events in your area. When I searched for events in just one Philadelphia zip code, I got forty-six matches.
- *Find mentors within your current company.* Talk to your superiors about their experiences and mistakes so you can learn

while you're still at your current job. You never know when such a conversation will lead to future business.

You might not need to start your business in motion by doing something so drastic; many entrepreneurs start their companies slowly over months or years while keeping a job and working on the new venture in evenings and on weekends. If that works for you, bravo! But if not, and you need an extra kick of motivation—like the kid in school who waits to start the paper the night before it's due (something I used to do myself)—consider this more drastic step. The entrepreneurs I've spoken to about "making the jump" have all said it was one of the most empowering, exciting times of their lives. Adrenaline does wonders, and feeling uncomfortable often increases your ability to perform.

Lessons Learned

- ► Nobody knows everything about starting and running a business at the outset.
- ► The best way to learn is to rely on the knowledge of others.
- ► Partnerships are nothing to fear as long as you find people who complement your strengths and weaknesses and give them "skin in the game."
- ► There is no substitute for face-to-face networking.
- ► If you know the right questions to ask, you will get more from every mentor relationship.
- ► If you remain unmotivated but still dream about entrepreneurship, you should consider jumping out of the plane.

The Next Twenty-Four

In the next twenty-four hours . . .

✓ Start a business plan outline if you think you need one.
✓ Make a list of five people in your area who have started successful businesses as well as where you'll take them to eat.
✓ Write down your questions for these people.
✓ Make a list of your business strengths and weaknesses.
✓ Start writing down the names of people you know who might bring strengths to your company that you need.
✓ Plan who might become part of your mastermind group.
✓ Go to LaunchersCafe.com, register, and post your request for potential partners on our Café Blogs.

My Dream Plan, Part 1

Describe your business in detail and how you will bring it into being.

My vision:

_____

_____

_____

_____

The lifestyle it will help me create:

_____

_____

_____

_____

The market need I will fill:

_____

_____

_____

_____

The first five things I will do to start:

_____

_____

_____

_____

The name and mission statement of my business:

_____

_____

_____

_____

"What if everyone tells me I can't do it?"

2

Pablo Picasso said, "I am always doing things I can't do. That's how I get to do them." I love that statement. In 1961, Beatles manager Brian Epstein had arranged many auditions for the Fab Four with record companies in London. Remember: these were the days before CDs and the internet, so bands who wanted to be signed to a recording contract had to audition live before record company executives. Several companies turned the Beatles away, including Columbia, and on January 2, 1962, they performed a fifteen-song audition for Decca Records consisting of mostly cover songs with a few Lennon and McCartney compositions sprinkled in. No one is certain which person made the decision to say no to the biggest-selling musical group of all time, but Decca got back to the band a few days later with the famous rejection line "Guitar groups are on the way out." The band signed with Parlophone a few months later, and you know the rest.

What was going on there? To be fair, it wasn't like the Beatles were doing "I Saw Her Standing There" or "Come Together," which would surely have set the Decca people on their ears. But how could anyone not recognize the talent and energy that would lead the lads from Liverpool to superstardom? I think in part it's because of what I call "innovation aversion." Our brains are wired to think in a straight line and to rely on the things that have worked for us in the past. We are conditioned to "play it safe."

Look at business. Original and innovative thinking and a daring spirit are what make billionaires and change industries. But most people don't have the ability to recognize the virtues of an internet platform, a company, or a rock group that's unlike anything that came before it. They actually recoil from white-hot new ideas and react with fear. I consider this an ironclad rule:

World-changing ideas are always introduced with the words "That will never work."

Picasso's style was so unnerving to the staid art world that when the National Gallery in London organized the first major postwar Picasso show in England, one newspaper wrote that his art was "the work of the devil" and was not fit for public exhibition in England. Even great minds fall into the trap of dismissing the daringly original: President Woodrow Wilson said, "It is ridiculous to think the motor car will someday replace the horse and buggy." Fortunately, we have also always had individuals who understood the tension between innovation and the fear of it. For example, it was Albert Einstein who said, "Great spirits have always encountered violent opposition from mediocre minds."

When They Call You Crazy, It May Be a Reason to Celebrate

When people tell you that your idea for a business is crazy, impossible, or foolish, they're not trying to be cruel or wishing for your failure. They're just being human. Most people fear visionary thinking because we are creatures of the familiar. If something worked in the past, then in our minds, only something similar can work in the future. As author Arthur Koestler said, "Creativity is the defeat of habit by originality." Many people pooh-poohed the idea of tourist trips into space. Now Virgin Galactic is staging test flights and preparing to take the wealthy into orbit.

Just about every idea that ever turned an industry upside down or minted a generation of new millionaires was considered crazy by the majority. That is, until it became a huge success. Then its value was suddenly obvious to all the naysayers! The moral of the story is that when you tell people—and this includes other entrepreneurs and businesspeople, who are as susceptible to innovation aversion as anybody else—about your vision and they snap, "Can't be done," don't lose faith. In fact, having someone tell you that your concept is bonkers can be reason to dance, sing, and plan for your initial public stock offering. The real currency in business is not money but original thinking.

Don't believe me? Look at the billionaire moguls of the world. They're not the people who write code for new software. They're the people who have the ideas. Steve Jobs probably hasn't written a line of code in years, but his ideas have reshaped Apple; produced the iMac, iPod, and iPhone; and resurrected a brand that was on the verge of disappearing just a few years ago. Creative, daring ideas change lives and reshape the world. **Creativity equals capital.**

Russell Simmons, for example, cofounded the Def Jam record label and helped define not only contemporary hip-hop and the hip-hop lifestyle, but created an entire industry around hip-hop music, clothing, and entertainment that permeates modern American culture. His ideas have created millionaires and thousands of jobs. So when you sit down with a friend over a cup of coffee (perhaps at your local Starbucks—another idea that originally got the "It will never work" stamp) and share your passionate idea for a new company, and she tells you that you're nuts, you may want to rejoice.

Agile Enough to Dodge the Fire Hose

Introducing a fresh new idea into the world is like being a nail that sticks up a bit: others are going to grab a hammer and try to pound you into conformity. **Being an entrepreneur means, in part, knowing when to listen and when not to listen to what others say.** It is vital that you know how much importance to give the opinions of other people. Keep in mind, they don't know your heart, share your vision, or feel your passion; do not allow their negative opinions to discourage you. Instead, use them as a source of inspiration. A flood of critical comments is commonly known as "firehosing." You've got to be able to dodge the water from that hose, or it will flatten you. Eventually, you will become strong enough to withstand the pressure of the water.

However, when someone you respect listens to your idea and, instead of firing back an instant "That's crazy," furrows his brow, thinks for a minute, and then brings up some specific questions or objections, it's foolish to stick your fingers in your ears and go, "La-la-la-la!" (It's also rude.) Reflexive dismissal and doubt as a result of ignorance should be ignored. Smart, practical advice from someone who knows what he or she is talking about should be heeded. Even if it's unsolicited, listen. If you're new at this and the person sitting across from you has a great deal of business experience, he or she might see a fatal flaw in your idea that you would never have seen. Take notes, ask questions, and in addition to getting advice on where your idea could go wrong, get some solutions. Don't let your ego keep you from rethinking a good idea and making it better. The people who survive and thrive in any economy are the ones willing to change their business plan—or their entire business model—on a dime. That's agility.

Agility is one of the hallmarks of a great entrepreneur. Two years ago, magazines and broadcast media wanted only high-end handbags, so we created a high-end line just to get them to talk about us. Now, most of the magazines only want to talk about bags under $50, so we've created a limited-style line that costs about $50. That wasn't part of my original plan, but thank God we did it. We started putting the strategy together in 2008 when the economy first started hurting. If we hadn't done that—if I had been too egotistical or stubborn to flex with the times and change course—we would be in a lot of trouble right now. Don't fall so in love with your idea that you won't change it in the face of good advice or new information.

Surround Yourself with Other Musicians

Listen to great jazz: Miles Davis, Charlie Parker, Coleman Hawkins, and others. What do you hear? Improvisation. You feel the music and go where it takes you. Entrepreneurship is the same way: you're often forced to improvise and innovate on the fly based on nothing more than instinct. That's another reason it's important to be careful who you listen to when your business idea is young and fragile. The bebop of Parker and Davis doesn't appeal to everyone; when it first appeared in the mid-1940s, guitarist and bandleader Eddie Condon said disdainfully, "They flat their fifths. We drink ours!" But today, the jazz of that era is considered the most incredible, challenging, and transformative of the century.

Jazz is also about passion, and the surest way to keep your belief in your idea strong is to make sure that you are passionately in love with it. You should adore your vision of what life will be like once you start your company. You're going to work harder than you ever have in your life, and the only way you will put in the long hours is if you love what you do.

Passion is my fuel. I can't wait for Mondays. Sunday night I get excited that the next day I get to work on my dream again! Then I get on Facebook and see so many people dreading Monday, saying the adult equivalent of "I don't want to go to school!" That negative energy is contagious; stay away from it. One of the best ways to thrive as an entrepreneur is to surround yourself with other entrepreneurs who have a positive influence on you. If you're a jazz musician, you hang out with other musicians because they help you polish your solos. If you're risking it all to launch something unique and brave, don't spend time with people who engage in defeatist thinking.

The friends I connect with are the ones who can't wait for Monday. When you surround yourself with these kinds of people, it helps you overcome your fears and stay in a state of inspiration. One of my friends works in a high-profile job in the media. People look at him and think, "Wow, he's got the life!" But every time he sees me, he asks excitedly, "What are you working on?" He wants to come to my side of the world. He likes to be around me because he likes that I support his vision. He tells me, "Every time I see you on Facebook, your comments are always positive, and you inspire me to want more from my life!" If you can find someone whose attitude inspires you to want more, then start spending more time with him or her.

Dreamer's Corner: A New Entrepreneur Q&A

Dhana Cohen, Founder/President
www.thenextbigzing.com
thenextbigzing@gmail.com

1. What is the name of your new business, and when did you start it?
The Next Big Zing, www.thenextbigzing.com. I started working on the idea in mid-2007, just launching the site in 2009.

2. What type of business is it?
It's a website dedicated to showcasing incredible artists and inventors through video reviews and infomercials, and also linking to their sites so consumers can purchase their goods. We make commissions by affiliate links to their sites and advertising revenue.

3. What was the greatest obstacle you faced in starting your business, and how did you overcome it?

The fear of failing. . . . I had tried so many other ideas before, and it's in my heart and soul to be an entrepreneur, so I finally said, "Let's make this idea happen without giving in!" It has been awe-inspiring, and I love having the reinforcement from clients who are so honored and thrilled to be a part of our site! So, yes, I did overcome it!

4. What has the experience of being an entrepreneur taught you about yourself, and how has it changed you?

It has taught me so much: that I can work for myself and dedicate my time to something that I love, to appreciate my creativity, and that I can create a business from scratch. It has taught me that no matter how many ups and downs I face, I can find ways to actually make it work, even if it wasn't the original way. I think it has made me a harder worker; when it's your business, you make it happen, no matter what time of day or night.

5. What is the most important lesson you have learned about starting a business?

To never let the naysayers talk you out of your dream.

6. Where is your business today as far as earnings, size, etc.? What are your prospects for the future?

Zero and proud; we're just launching. The prospects are huge. Who wouldn't want to find a great gift and watch someone show it to you online? It's the new entertainment of internet shopping!!

What if *your idea does work?*

This is the simplest mental 180-degree turn of all time. When someone tells you, "Oh, that idea will never work," say in return, "Yes, but what if it does?" We are so programmed to think first of how something can go wrong that it's a shock to think about the idea that they might go right. If you have a backup plan to handle what might go wrong, you're going to need it. I'm good at thinking on my feet. I don't waste time on hypothetical situations.

You've heard this: **eighty percent of new businesses fail in the first five years**. A thousand business writers have quoted it as gospel. But just because something is repeated a great deal doesn't make it true. This "fact" is a myth. In his book *The Illusions of Entrepreneurship: The Costly Myths that Entrepreneurs, Investors, and Policy Makers Live By*, author Scott Shane highlights a special tabulation done by the Bureau of the Census for the Office of Advocacy of the U.S. Small Business Administration. The data show the average ten-year survival rate of businesses started in 1992 across all sectors. By 1997, 45 percent were still in business. Even after ten years, nearly 30 percent were still surviving. And as Shane points out, the figures have remained consistent to today.

So you've got nearly a fifty-fifty chance of making it! I would argue that one of the reasons so many small businesses fail is not because the ideas behind them are not good, but because the creators accept the 80 percent failure myth and have one foot in the grave before they ever get started. If you assume that you're going to fail right off the bat, you're going to plan halfheartedly, broadcast a negative message to potential partners, and fail to put in the work. In mentoring entrepreneurs, I have noticed a few common qualities among people whose businesses fail shortly after launch:

- They apologize for their idea.
- Other people can easily talk them into changing it.
- They find reasons to delay instead of finding reasons to act.
- They fear risk.
- They fear being out of their comfort zone.

As I've said before, mind-set is the biggest obstacle for most entrepreneurs. If your mind-set is not right and you are not constantly monitoring and controlling it, you'll get steamrolled. A crucial self-management skill I try to pass on to the would-be entrepreneurs I meet with is to gain some perspective on what they are trying to do. It's very common for fearful entrepreneurs to dismiss their idea by saying things like, "Oh, it's just a small business." But it's not. Entrepreneurs change the world. Entrepreneurship, innovation, and job creation are noble endeavors. Remembering that what you do is important is part of keeping yourself motivated. Don't forget to look at the big picture from time to time.

One of these days, I'm going to poll entrepreneurs who have and haven't been successful, and I'm going to ask them how much time they spend managing their companies and how much time they spend managing their thinking. I'll bet the results will show that the most successful ones spent at least half their time keeping themselves positive, staying motivated in the face of setbacks, and doing things that fueled their passions.

Why not use people's criticism and naysaying to make your idea better?

There are three ways to react to the negative opinions that we hear when we present a unique business idea:

1. Be discouraged by them.
2. Ignore them.
3. Leverage them.

I believe in #3. Soliciting opinions is like panning for gold: you're going to get a lot of rocks and dirt for every nugget of wisdom that you can actually use. But every now and then, someone's "It won't work" response will contain some real wisdom that you can put to use. Winston Churchill said, "Criticism may not be agreeable, but it is necessary. It fulfills the same function as pain in the human body. It calls attention to an unhealthy state of things." Occasionally, a critical comment will bring your attention to a flaw in your plan.

For example, a gentleman wanted to start a company that created a karaoke machine that would link up to the iPod. A cool and creative idea, but when he told a friend about it, the friend was dubious about the cost of manufacturing the products. Instead of being angry or discouraged, the entrepreneur sat down and rethought his concept. His new business model was simple: instead of building the karaoke boxes, he would license the technology to other companies! He did just that and now has a thriving small company based on inventions and intellectual property—not manufacturing—that reduces risk, cost, and chaos.

Constructive criticism is like having a personal trainer. A good trainer pushes you, works you until your muscles are sore, and makes you give up your favorite junk food but, in the end, you're better off. When you know who and what to listen to, you can turn negative reactions into new strategies. The doubts of other people can fire you up.

What if your idea is so unique that you will have no competition because you've created a new category of business?

It's one thing to open yet another Italian restaurant in New York; if you're going to do that, you'd better have deep pockets, an incredible chef, and a lot of luck. But if you come up with a new kind of cuisine or a new way of delivering it, then you may have no competitors. Naysayers might snicker and say, "Sure, that's because no one wants that product/service/experience." But if you can take a thrilling, original idea that appeals to people and get it in front of them, you can create demand.

Kogi Korean BBQ-To-Go is an excellent example of this. It's a company that has three Korean barbecue taco trucks that cruise around Los Angeles selling fantastic fusion cuisine to the city's multicultural population. The catch: nobody knows where the trucks will be until they send out an alert via their Twitter feed. Then young Angelenos come running and have been known to line up for two hours to get the food at three o'clock in the morning. Not only did these guys take a food concept and make it mobile, they found a way to promote it that no one was using.

Your idea could actually create a new business model and a new industry. Apple did it when they developed the iPod. They didn't want to be just another MP3 player, so they created another product that they could market with the iPod to make the iPod a blockbuster: iTunes. Now iTunes is a leader in music sales, and this business model has made iPod the fastest-selling music player in history. Ford Motor Company didn't just start mass-producing cars. They also bought out trolley systems, paved roads, and built their own rubber plantations. They transformed the world around them to make their product necessary. Sometimes an original business model, not a product, changes everything.

Do you have competition? Here are some ways to find out:

- Create Google alerts to send you news about ideas similar to yours.
- Read print and online trade publications to see what new companies are in the works.
- Pay attention to venture capital news and trend-spotting business websites like Springwise.com.
- Network. Keep your ear to the ground, and develop sources at venture firms and in the trade press.

But most of all, if you find out that your idea is so new that you have little or no competition, be happy. That's great. It gives you a short window of time to consolidate your position without having to look over your shoulder.

What if the craziest ideas are usually the most successful ones?

It's fascinating to see successful people who are still reluctant to be the first to market with something new. They won't take the risk. **Well, nothing great is ever achieved without risk.** For example, I went into a meeting to pitch a new show idea to a TV network. I surrounded myself with a very successful production team, so the network knew I could deliver the goods. I made my pitch, and the production manager said to me, "No one wants this right now." I said, "So you want what everyone else is pitching? I came in here with something original." If you need proof that the mainstream entertainment business is more interested in carbon copies than originality, just look at summer movies. What do you see? Sequel after sequel.

The "crazy" ideas always end up being the ones that capture people's imaginations, get attention, and become megahits. According to Mark Burnett's book *Jump In! Even If You Don't Know How to Swim*, no one wanted *Survivor* when he first pitched it. He got turned down at least six times. Yet this was the show that completely changed the face of television forever, because Mark showed that reality TV could produce blockbusters. **No one was looking for *Survivor* when it came along.** Everyone says they want the next big thing, but what most people are really looking for is a clone of what somebody else did with enough changes made that they don't get sued. Originality is risky. It's scary. That's why everyone is always copying everyone else. But that's not how you become great.

Mark Burnett went back to Les Moonves, who was then CEO of Viacom, and took a cover of *Time* magazine on which he had superimposed himself and Moonves and added a caption that said something like, "Mark Burnett and CBS change the face of television." I think Moonves said yes just out of admiration for Burnett's sheer moxie. But in the end, Mark Burnett had the last laugh. Now, after *Survivor, The Apprentice*, and more, he's got an empire.

Don't worry if your idea seems implausible, defies conventional wisdom, and makes people look at you like you have a screw loose. Worry if it doesn't.

Why not think up a pitch that will appeal to potential partners who are as innovative and creative as you?

The power of that crazy, first-to-market idea is that it will attract other wildly creative entrepreneurs. The world of start-ups has a very low signal-to-noise ratio: a lot of noise, very little signal. Even the people who are most adept at risk taking become jaded, and it takes a lot to grab their attention. Truly original ideas have the power to cut through the noise and make smart, talented people sit up and take notice. But you've got to be able to pitch your idea to them in a way that captures their passion.

Eric Bolling, with whom I do Fox News's *The Strategy Room* every Thursday afternoon, also cohosts a show called *Fox Business Happy Hour*. On this show, Eric and his cohosts have a segment called "So You Think You're an Entrepreneur," in which people come on and pitch their ideas and Eric and his cohosts tell them whether or not they would invest in them. Try watching this show, and find out if you have what it takes (among other things, a great idea, a well-thought-out branding strategy, and limitless passion and self-belief). It's a great tool for becoming better at pitching.

When you're pitching to creative minds, know what you're looking for. Are you after possible equity partners who would join your new company from the ground floor? Investors? People with their own companies who might do a joint venture with you? Marketing geniuses? Financial wizards? Sales experts? Once you know what's on your shopping list, develop your pitch and focus on the originality of your idea and the "market outcomes." Acknowledge that what you're proposing is daring and a bit risky but that those are its strengths. Creative, innovative people love risks.

Don't make a PowerPoint presentation. Talk. In person. If you like, create a cool website for your idea, protect it with a temporary password, and after your talk, invite your audience to visit the site for more details. But it's going to be your enthusiasm and passion that communicate the brilliance of your idea and get other pioneering people as excited about the business as you are.

Why not join a community designed for start-ups and entrepreneurs that can support you as you develop your wild idea?

There's an entire online ecosystem devoted to start-ups and entrepreneurship. After all, today's internet was created by audacious entrepreneurs! I created Launchers Café because I wanted ongoing interaction with members throughout all stages of their companies' growth, so I and other members could support them when they began to doubt their ideas. When someone wonders, "How can I get my products in a swag suite?" she posts her question, and before long, several members usually respond with some helpful answers. It's a productive, supportive ongoing conversation.

Looking at a business magazine, you can get inspired and excited, but you have all these questions and no way to get them answered. There is distance between you and the people who have been there, done that. I created the Launchers Café model so that entrepreneurs could get their questions answered by people who are just as creative as they are and who are experiencing the same fears, doubts, and excitement, regardless of their past levels of achievement.

When you're carrying around a "crazy" idea in your head, joining a community of like-minded people helps you sustain momentum to continue after the inspiration fades and you get down to the real work. It also helps you feel like you're not alone. Ladies Who Launch (ladieswholaunch.com) is another great example of a place to find people and resources. They have monthly meetings and provide e-mail blasts of useful content for members. YoungEntrepreneur.com, i-genius.org, and StartupNation.com are also excellent online business communities.

When you're connected with a community, you're going to learn much more than you bargained for. People might be talking about how to get sponsors for a website, how to get retailers to carry products, or how to generate publicity. Networking with other creative minds gives you the chance to talk to your peers and see how they did it: how they proposed the proposal, how they took the first call, how they got the meeting. When you're sailing unknown seas, it helps to be with others who are in the same boat—these fellow travelers could also introduce you to the exact people you need to be talking to.

Lessons Learned

- ► Most responses to your vision will be based on fear and doubt. That's human nature.
- ► Most of us doubt any truly original idea that comes along.
- ► Being told, "Your idea is crazy" may be the perfect compliment, because it means your idea is original and evokes a passionate response in people.
- ► The most successful companies are those based on paradigm-shaking, audacious ideas.
- ► Business is like jazz: it demands improvisation and agility.

▶ Spending time with other entrepreneurs will defuse the power of negative thinking and encourage constant inspiration.

▶ Your idea might just work.

▶ Sometimes, having a crazy idea means you're being innovative: you could be the first one to think of something and will have no competitors at first.

The Next Twenty-Four

In the next twenty-four hours . . .

✓ Start a journal cataloging all the feedback you get about your business idea, what it means, and how you can turn negatives into positives.

✓ Identify at least one online start-up entrepreneur's networking group you can join.

✓ Develop a draft of your pitch—the one you will use to promote your idea to other creative, visionary people.

✓ List the individuals with whom you will not share your idea until your company is already established, because you want to avoid the toxin of their negative thinking; this will keep you from being tempted in a moment of excitement and inspiration.

My Dream Plan, Part 2

Set your goals for your first year.

Goals for what I want to earn:

_____

_____

_____

_____

Goals for my lifestyle:

_____

_____

_____

_____

Goals for who I want to become:

_____

_____

_____

_____

Goals for how I want my business to impact others:

_____

_____

_____

_____

"What if I'm terrified of losing my job security?"

3

You've put together the plan for your new retail store, the one you've been dreaming about since the kids started school. You have the whole thing pretty well worked out: what you'll stock, who you'll source your merchandise from, and even your first social media campaign. You've finished your business plan and run the numbers in QuickBooks, and they look good. You feel ready to make the big jump, to become a self-employed entrepreneur. Who knows? In a year you might even be able to hire one or two people from the community! How great would it feel to create some jobs for others or even win some "best of" awards? How wonderful would it be to inspire others to start their own businesses in the same way that earlier entrepreneurs probably inspired you?

You decide that on Monday you will give your notice at work and turn the page. You go to bed looking forward to a weekend of excited planning. Then you find you're having trouble falling asleep. When you do finally nod off, you wake in a cold sweat. For a while, you can't figure out why, but then you realize that you're terrified down to your bones about leaving the safe harbor of your

WHAT IF? & WHY NOT?

9-to-5 job. No matter how hard you work, there's still no guarantee that you'll survive week to week. Are you making a huge mistake in saying good-bye to steady pay and health benefits? Sure, you'll still be on your spouse's or parents' insurance, but what about college and retirement savings? What if your spouse gets laid off?

Suddenly this doesn't look like such a great idea. You're scared to death of living "without a net," and you're considering just forgetting all about your dream. Maybe you could revisit the idea after the kids go off to college in thirteen or fourteen years, but for now, maybe it would be safer if you stayed where you are.

Real Job Security

When the economy is shaky or struggling, no job is truly secure. A layoff can seemingly happen without warning. Lots of people lose their jobs or are at risk of being laid off, but is spending months trying to find another job in which they have no control really their only option?

For many people who lose their jobs, getting another job is the only option that enters their minds. Never mind that clocking in and clocking out is inherently unfulfilling; many people are brainwashed into thinking that's their only option. Some never even consider the possibility that they could become their own bosses. They equate self-employment with insecurity.

Well, let's face it: there is no real security in anything in this life. The best you can do is give yourself the most knowledge, the best relationships, and the strongest preparation possible so that no matter what happens, you land on your feet. That's not going to happen while you're working for someone else. But when you're faced with unemployment and maybe a tough job market, you can't afford to be complacent anymore. You have to become tough, smart, and opportunistic. What choice do you have?

Let me share a harsh truth with you: **your employer has to care about numbers and the bottom line first**. The people who run your company have to prioritize quarterly profits, stock options, and share price. **The only one watching out for your interests is you.** So if you've lost your job or are worried that you're going to be the next one getting a pink slip, I implore you to see the possibilities in working for yourself—even if it is something on the side. Don't run to the next safe harbor of another employer before you consider whether you really can strike out on your own as a consultant or freelancer.

Yes, the idea is a little scary. It was scary for me to commit so much money to the Butler Bag Company without knowing if it would work, but I was motivated, because I really believed in my idea and was tired of missing out on opportunities for success. More than that, I knew ahead of time that the experience was going to make me feel uneasy and that the feeling had nothing to do with my idea or my ability to make my business profitable. **The fear you feel is nothing more than your psychological reaction to being outside your comfort zone.** It feels comforting and safe to let someone else worry about where the money is coming from and to collect a paycheck every two weeks. You're not the one most responsible for the business succeeding or failing. That feels like security—until you realize that you have little or no real control!

As best-selling author Brian Tracy points out in *Getting Rich Your Own Way*, 74 percent of self-made millionaires in America made their fortunes by starting their own companies. Why wouldn't you consider starting your own company? Until you are fully in control of your lifestyle, your income, and your future, you're really at the mercy of other people and outside forces.

Dreamer's Corner: A New Entrepreneur Q&A

Dell Trahan, Cofounder
www.tkmobiledetail.com
tkmobiledetail@yahoo.com

1. What is the name of your new business, and when did you start it?

T & K's Mobile Detailing & Pressure Washing started September 1, 2006 (this is a mother/son business). T & K's stands for Tammy and Kristina. My son's wife, Tammy, and stepdaughter, Kristina, were both murdered four years ago. So we are building a family legacy for the two remaining daughters, who are seven and eighteen years old. When we make our *Fortune 500* cover, the article will read "From Tragedy to Triumph."

2. What type of business is it?

Mobile car/fleet detailing and pressure washing.

3. What was the greatest obstacle you faced in starting your business, and how did you overcome it?

Quitting corporate America, using my last $300 to buy a piece of equipment, and not having any more unemployment benefits to take care of our personal bills. I overcame it by stepping out on faith, believing God would make a way and open up some doors. And He did!

4. What has the experience of being an entrepreneur taught you about yourself, and how has it changed you?

I can do anything that I put my mind to and that I believe in. Now I know the sky is the limit. I haven't changed at all, because I have always been a hard, dedicated, and faithful worker. I knew when I was twenty-three years old that I would one day have my own business. I didn't know what it would be, but I knew I didn't always want to work for someone else.

5. What is the most important lesson you have learned about starting a business?

There are so many avenues, people, organizations that are out here to help small businesses succeed. You just have to want it badly enough and get out here and work hard.

6. Where is your business today as far as earnings, size, etc.? What are your prospects for the future?

The first year we did about $25,000, and the second year we did about $110,000. The future will have us franchising all over the world.

What if the price of being secure and comfortable is being unhappy?

My mom had a TV show when I was a kid, and I would appear as the kids' commentator, which I loved until it resulted in my peers ridiculing me whenever I made a mistake. But when I complained about how uncomfortable this made me, Mom would say, "If you weren't uncomfortable today, you didn't grow today." I still live by that idea. Years later, before I launched the Butler Bag, vendors at QVC asked me to become an on-air guest and sell products for other companies. I was scared to death of doing it. They asked me again and again, and again and again I said no.

Can you imagine me, someone who, today, is in the business of creating and promoting consumer brands, turning down an opportunity to appear on the world's most successful home shopping program in front of millions and millions of viewers? I almost wasted that incredible chance. But then I heard my mother's voice saying, "If you weren't uncomfortable today, you didn't grow today." That convinced me. I knew I couldn't let my irrational fear prevent me from seizing a career-changing moment. So I went on QVC and did well, and it was a springboard for my career. Facing and overcoming that fear gave me the confidence to start the Butler Bag Company. Now I'm on TV all the time, and it's one of my favorite things to do.

When you're facing the choice between looking for another job after a layoff or striking out on your own as a freelancer, you're facing the same issue: getting far outside your comfort zone. Unfortunately, schools don't teach us the skills we need to work for ourselves. We're taught to "get a job." I disagree with this. I think part of the standard curriculum should be entrepreneurship and self-employment. It won't be for everyone, and that's fine. The world needs people who can thrive while working for someone else, too, and not everyone is cut out to be an independent contractor. But given the joy you can experience and the financial rewards you can realize, I think everyone should know the basics and be able to make up his or her mind with open eyes.

I've talked with thousands of entrepreneurs, and many of them have told me that one of the times they find most exciting is when they *lose* a client, because finding new business challenges their skill and knowledge and makes them grow exponentially. You will feel the same way. When times are tough, you will become smarter and tougher and happier.

What if being in control of your income gave you more security than ever?

Alongside the exhilaration of being independent comes the fear that the buck stops with you. Can you keep finding new business? Can you pay your own bills? That's frightening if you're not used to trusting your ability. But once you get into that new comfort zone of self-reliance, you're going to find out that it feels *exhilarating* to be your own boss. So many of my friends who are entrepreneurs say the same thing: it was the scariest thing they ever did, but now they wouldn't trade it for the world.

A huge part of that satisfaction comes from knowing that you are creating your own security by being in control of your intellectual property, your growth, and your opportunities. You decide what new clients to pursue. You own the rights to your inventions or the things you write. You're the one with the power to make licensing deals, collect royalties, or bring on investors. Not only do you choose to pursue new opportunities and go after new business, but you can choose how much you earn and how much time you spend working. Do you want to simply replace the income you had at your old job while working at home and being with your kids? Great. Do you want to build a company and employ a hundred people? Do it. Do you want to be a freelance consultant and pull down $250,000 a year by writing a best seller and going on the speaking circuit? It's your call.

In the end, the best job and income security is what have the power and confidence to create, because no one can pull it out from under you. Having the skills that entrepreneurs possess makes you more agile and resilient, giving you a greater sense of control of your destiny. When you're the one making the decisions, no one can lay you off. No one can make strategic decisions that you disagree with or choose partners you don't trust. You have control, and before long, you will get to the point where, when business slumps, you lose a client, or some other trouble arises, you say, "No problem. I'll get through this. I always do."

Why not save a financial cushion?

ABC News personal finance expert Mellody Hobson writes, "I believe you cannot be a part-time entrepreneur. The most successful entrepreneurs are those who stop what they are doing and focus only on their business (think Bill Gates and Ted Turner). That said, if you are going to leave your job to start a business, you need to make sure you have built a substantial financial cushion or have lined up enough investors to get you through the lean years. Keep in mind, starting a business is very similar to building or remodeling a home—it will likely cost you a lot more money than you originally planned."

I agree with this, though as I pointed out earlier, you can start some businesses for as little as $50. If your business can't get off the ground so inexpensively, one of the best ways to give yourself some peace of mind is to save some money as a safety net. Eventually, being your own boss will give you the financial control you desire, but in the meantime, it's nice to have some capital saved, so you can survive while business is ramping up. I would recommend that anyone planning to leave full-time employment to launch his own business have at least three months of household expenses saved (aside from the capital he needs to operate his business) before he takes the plunge. Six months' worth is even better. If you're "bootstrapping" (using your own money from savings, selling things you own, or using your salary from your job to fund your business), you will have to establish some new habits. This is what I recommend:

- Set a total savings goal and then divide by the amount of money you can put away each month. That will tell you how long you need to save before you can give your notice at work. So if your family's average monthly expenses come to $3,000, you need to save at least $9,000 to be safe. If you decide you can put away $1,000 a month, you'll need to save and be patient for nine months before you're ready to launch your company full time (though you can certainly start it part time whenever you're ready).
- Set up a monthly auto-transfer from your checking account into a special new business nest egg savings account. That

way you won't even have the temptation to spend that money "just this month" because it will go into your "safety net" account without you even thinking about it.

- Don't let your engine idle while you're saving. This is pre-launch time, one of the most critical periods for a new business. You can be networking, attending events and developing key relationships, setting up your presence on Facebook and Twitter, developing new product or service offerings, and even making sales online (if possible). You can also test your business without as much criticism or expectations. Early customers can be a phenomenal focus group. Use this time to lay your foundation. Remember that you don't want the need to save to turn into an excuse for inaction.

- When you've got your "safety net" money saved, don't just toast your success. Take the next step, which is to quit your job and devote yourself full time to your idea. Keep your excited edge.

Why not talk about your plans with trusted friends and family?

Many novice entrepreneurs get cold feet because they're afraid that their families won't support their walking away from a steady income. But if you have an honest passion for what you want to do and a solid plan for continuing to earn income to support your loved ones, odds are your family is going to be behind you 110 percent. But you won't know until you talk to them.

If motivation is a problem, there's nothing like telling others about what you plan to do to make you accountable. None of us wants to be asked a year after we announce our grand scheme, "So, did you start that business you told me about?" and to turn red-faced and mutter, "No, I never got around to it." As I discussed in reference to mastermind groups, telling people about your ideas and dreams turns everyone in your life into a kind of accidental coach ready to hold you responsible for your own aspirations.

When I was in the fitness world, I was a master aerobics instructor and trainer, and I wanted to compete on a national level, but I was afraid that if I failed, my clients wouldn't think I was a good instructor. I decided that the only way I was going to do it was if I told other people about it and gave myself no choice but to follow through. So in 1999, I decided I was going to compete in the National Aerobics Championship and Galaxy Fitness Competition in the spring of 2000. I told my clients and colleagues about my dream, and you know what happened? I had trainers wanting to help me with my gymnastics component and sponsors wanting to help pay my way. I was able to follow through on my longtime dream.

Sometimes friends can wake you up to the possibilities. My friend Tracy was working at a big PR firm when she was laid off. She immediately started looking for another job even though she had tons of clients who adored her. Finally, I said, "Tracy, why don't you just start your own agency?" She had gotten locked into the "I have to work for someone else" mind-set and didn't even see the incredible opportunity right in front of her. Once I called it to her attention, she caught fire. She started her own firm and brought in great clients, and now she's working harder than ever and loving her life more than she ever thought possible.

What if your employer supported your going out on your own?

I met my friend Meredith Applebaum a few years ago while she was the talent producer for *The Big Idea with Donny Deutsch*, a show I appeared on many times. Meredith loved working with CNBC and Donny, but one day she was talking to Donny about her dream to start an image consulting business. Donny could tell it was something she was really excited about, and he said to her, "Why don't you do it?" Meredith looked at him like he was crazy and said, "I can't! I have a job and have bills to pay!"

Donny said, "Never say can't!" Remember: this was her own boss saying this, which I find extraordinary. On the spot, Donny gave Meredith a plan for how she was going to start her business while still working for him and grow it to a point where she could finally leave to start her dream! Man, how cool would it be if everyone worked for someone like that? Well, you never know. You may. You might be surprised at how supportive your boss and colleagues could be about your dream. If your boss has an entrepreneurial spirit, he or she will understand your desires and ambition and could be a huge asset, like Donny was for Meredith, in helping you get what you want.

Not every company is hostile to the idea of its people leaving to start their own companies. In a time when so many companies are being forced to downsize to survive, some actually welcome their people leaving on their own. It spares the employer the pain and potential legal hassles of a layoff and keeps relationships with employees on good terms. You might even become a customer of or vendor to your old employer!

If you suspect your company might be looking to let people go (or if they are already laying people off), it might be worth it to talk to your boss about your plans. Be honest and say, "I'm thinking seriously about starting my own company. I know you're trying to reduce headcount, and I'm wondering if we can't work something out that benefits you and me." You might find your superiors surprisingly supportive, even going to far as to give you ninety days with pay to plan your exit, a testimonial letter, or maybe even some suggestions for customers. You'll never know until you ask.

Why not ease your way into things by moonlighting?

Like Meredith, if you have a supportive employer, you may want to start moonlighting as a freelancer or consultant while you're still working, making your transition more emotionally comfortable and financially safe. You don't need a storefront or staff. All you need to do is let people know you're out there and figure out how to charge them. This is especially easy if you're in a service business such as PR, copywriting, design, or consulting.

Start asking around and capitalizing on your relationships to generate business. Spend ten hours a week slowly building up your "entrepreneur muscles" and earning a little extra money, and if the time comes that your job is obsolete—or you're lucky enough to decide for yourself to leave—the transition will be much more rewarding. Here are some tips:

- *Be honest with your employer.* In general, companies may be more concerned with their bottom line than their people, but most companies actually do want their employees to do well, and executives often admire those with the initiative to strike out on their own. Level with your boss, and as long as you keep current on your work at the office, you might find him or her 100 percent behind you.
- *Avoid "poaching."* Your employer might fear that you will contact its customers and steal them when you leave. Some customers might suspect the same thing and see you as dishonest or disloyal. So don't go after your company's customers. Find your own. At the same time, network and let the customers know your plans. If they like and respect you, they may recommend new clients to you down the road.
- *Know your services and fees.* Professionals offer a specific suite of services and know exactly what they charge. Don't

estimate. Don't say, "Oh, I do everything." Be specific about the services you offer and don't offer, and charge what you think you're worth. If you want, give new clients a special "introductory rate" to get their business, but let them know that, normally, you charge more.

Of course, the other issue is time. How do you work a full-time job, manage a family (if you have one), moonlight, and still have a life? It's not easy, but it can be done if you want it badly enough. Most people find that they have five to ten hours of extra time per week once they stop wasting it. Try some of these tips, and I'll bet you find the time you need to get your feet wet:

- *Set precise, incremental goals.* If the next big item on your to-do list is "develop website," then break that big goal down into smaller increments like "talk to Web designers" and "write online copy."
- *Delegate and collaborate.* Remember that you don't have to do it all alone. Ask your family or your friends to help you with tasks like preparing mailers, creating a home office, or doing research.
- *Beware of overscheduling yourself.* Most important tasks usually take twice as long to accomplish as you think.
- *Take care of yourself.* Sick time is "nothing gets done" time. One of your top priorities should be taking care of mind and body. My fitness and good health were critical when I launched the Butler Bag Company and then developed more new lifestyle brands, because I was constantly on the run and working sixteen-hour days. If I hadn't kept myself in good shape, I would have probably fallen apart physically. Eat a healthy diet, exercise four or five times a week, and try to do something that relieves stress, such as yoga or meditation.
- *Quit watching TV and Net surfing.* Curtail these activities unless they are crucial to your business. The average American

watches five hours of television per day. That's often wasted time.

Lessons Learned

► Fear of living without the security of a job is normal, but it just means you don't yet trust your ability to earn a living.
► The "security" of a full-time job is illusory, because you don't have control. The greatest security you'll ever have is when you control your growth and potential.
► Leaving a job to start your company will take you out of your comfort zone, and that will be nerve-wracking at first. But it will become the most exhilarating and self-fulfilling thing you have ever done and can make you an inspiration to others.
► It's fine to save a nest egg for safety or to try to launch your start-up while temporarily keeping your job. But take action; don't let the delay in leaving your job become an excuse for saying, "I'll get to it one day."
► Goal setting helps you focus your energy. Sharing your dreams with others allows them to both encourage you and give you a push when you need one.
► Delegation and collaboration will save your sanity.

The Next Twenty-Four

In the next twenty-four hours . . .

✓ Talk to your boss about your plans, and find out how and if your company will work with you.
✓ Calculate your monthly expenses, taking into account cutbacks you can make to minimize the strain on your finances.

✓ Talk with your family about whether leaving your job is an acceptable option at this time.

✓ Set your goals for the next year, insert them into an online organizer (try Yahoo! Calendar or Google Calendar, which are free), and discuss them with the people who are important in your life.

✓ Think about how great it will be when you are the boss and in control of what you do, how much you earn, and how you spend your time, while being an inspiration to others and loving what you do.

My Dream Plan, Part 3

List the people, technology, marketing, and finances you will need
to make your dream come true.

People:

_____

_____

_____

_____

Technology:

_____

_____

_____

_____

Marketing:

_____

_____

_____

_____

Finances:

_____

_____

_____

4

"What if someone steals my idea?"

Quick—who invented the telephone? Alexander Graham Bell, right? Wrong. Formerly secret files revealed by the British Science Museum in 2003 show that in 1863, thirteen years before Scotsman Bell got his patent, a German named Johann Philipp Reis had actually built a working prototype of a telephone. So why isn't Reis immortalized? Because the British suppressed their test results on his invention so their own Bell could get the patent and go down in history. Sometimes people do unscrupulous things. Credit goes to the wrong person. Ideas are stolen. But it's not very common. If the fear that some unscrupulous competitor will poach your brilliant concept is stopping you from launching your company, rest easy. Don't let that be an excuse not to live your dream, because there are many reasons why your idea is probably safe.

Reason 1: You Cannot Take the Visionary Out of the Vision

In 2000, Toyota rolled out the Prius, the first mass-produced, affordable hybrid car, and it was an instant hit. They sold hundreds of thousands of cars, and the Prius quickly became not only the bellwether of the new hybrid industry but a major status symbol on both the East and West Coasts. Anybody who was famous and eco-conscious drove one. Well, you would think other car companies would be ripping off the Prius left and right, wouldn't you? American carmakers debuted hybrid trucks, SUVs, and more, but they just haven't captured the imagination of the American driver like the Prius has. Today, not only does Prius "own" the hybrid car brand in the mind of the consumer, but other companies are turning to Toyota to license and use their hybrid technology.

What happened? Other car companies could manage the steel and batteries needed to manufacture *a* hybrid vehicle, but they could not duplicate Toyota's vision or their unique commitment to product and process improvement. It's the same way with every unique business idea, from an invention to a business model. **Your idea is who you are; it's an expression of your mind, inspiration, goals, personality, and life experiences, all of which are unique to you.** Although someone else could, in theory, duplicate the mechanical and operational details of your retail store or your new social networking website,

> **no one can run the business like you will,
> because there is no one like you.**

Ideas can be knocked off. There are other organizing handbags out there; I don't kid myself that the Butler Bag itself is unique. What's unique is the way I run my company, manage my people, build my brand, and bring new ideas to life. Vision and motivation can't be knocked off. You cannot take the visionary out of the vision. Once you do, you get a knockoff, and knockoffs are never the same as the original. The execution isn't the same. The message won't be the same. The brand won't be the same. If you move forward with that understanding—that you are the only you—you won't worry about idea theft. Stop fixating on your competition. Do what you have got to do. If you are a visionary, you will keep evolving. Because of that, anyone trying to ride your coattails will always be ten steps behind you.

Reason 2: No Competitor Will Have the Same People You Do

Your team will be an enormous factor in your success. From your financial expert to your marketing creatives to your webmaster, your team will be as unique as you are, so your company will express your vision—via everything from product development to customer service—in a way that's impossible to copy.

For instance, my management style is always centered on making myself and my people the happiest and best we can be. I have made the conscious decision to use each day's energy in a productive way. As a result, I strive for a company vibe that is very life-affirming and positive. If one of my employees has a problem, in our company culture, the approach is not only to state what the problem is, but also suggest a solution. That gets us all talking about solutions and, in the end, the problem stops being a problem and becomes a challenge to find the best solution. It's a much more positive, productive experience.

If I have people in my organization with self-sabotaging mindsets, they will undo a lot of the work that I do every day. That is the nature of the organization that I've created, and it's unique to me. Your company will be unique to you, because the people you hire will reflect your vision, and they will also be like no one else. That's why, although it's important to encourage individuals in your company to express their talents, it's just as vital to hire people who can appreciate and enact your overarching vision and even add to it. It's one more way to differentiate your brand.

Reason 3: Everyone Thinks His or Her Own Ideas Are Better at First

Nikola Tesla, the brilliant Serbian engineer and inventor, once said, "I do not think there is any thrill that can go through the human heart like that felt by the inventor as he sees some creation of the brain unfolding to success. . . . Such emotions make a man forget food, sleep, friends, love, everything." I understand perfectly what he was saying. We all fall in love with our own ideas, because they are like our children. I do it, you do it, all entrepreneurial spirits do. We thrive off creating.

This is to your advantage when you're trying to get a new business off the ground. Even if your idea is stunningly original and has the potential to take over a lucrative market or even create a new market, odds are that everyone will still think his or her own ideas are superior. That is, until your idea takes off and sets the world on fire. Then the pirates will come out of their hideouts, because you've proven the concept.

Reason 4: Very Few Entrepreneurs Really Want to Create Something New

That's why franchises are a $125 billion industry. Most people want the lifestyle that comes with working for themselves but not the risk that comes with creating something new out of thin air. Launching innovation takes massive effort and a real tolerance for risk. It's the difference between breaking trail in an uncharted wilderness and trekking over a well-worn path. When you're on a trail created by someone else, even though you're still having a wilderness experience, you're closer to your comfort zone, because you know someone has been there before you. Breaking new ground with no one to depend on but yourself isn't for everyone.

Even big corporations are averse to risk. Corporations won't steal your idea until you've proven it. They will sit back and watch for two or three years before they even think about making a move to buy you or try to crush you. (That's when it's nice to have a team of great lawyers on your side and a wall of intellectual property protection already in place.) In the end, the risk of idea theft is overrated. You will have already put in the hours to solve any problems that arise, and anyone who comes after you won't. This puts them at a huge disadvantage. This is why small companies who act boldly and creatively can often run rings around large corporations, which are traditionally very slow-moving.

Reason 5: There Is Room for Competitors in Any Market

What's the difference between an iPhone and a BlackBerry Curve? Not much in technology terms. But in terms of the brand, there's a world of difference. There are iPhone people and BlackBerry people. Both devices are massive best sellers, which proves that there is always room for more than one expression of the same idea in the same market—in this case, a touch-screen mobile phone and minicomputer.

What makes this possible is the brand. I talk about branding extensively in Chapter 7, and that's because your brand is the most important thing you have. Similar products can all be successful in the same market, because their brands appeal to different buyers. Take Lexus, Mercedes, and BMW. They all produce fabulous luxury cars, and there's not a lot of difference between them. But their unique brands attract a certain kind of customer who stays loyal for years. HP and Dell computers are almost identical except for a few tweaks to the case design and the name badge; it's their brands that diverge, and those brands allow them to capture their own segments of the marketplace.

Your company or product will have its own brand, and because of that, there's room for you and the competition. The Butler Bag appeals to a certain type of woman, and other kinds of bags are catnip to other kinds of shoppers. As long as I protect my brand and ensure that it remains consistent and likable, there's plenty of room for my company and others to share the market.

Prudent or Paranoid?

This is not to say that you should be blithe about protecting your intellectual property. You should definitely play your cards close to the vest when you have a brand-new idea that hasn't been brushed with even a light layer of legal protection. However, there is a fine line between prudent business confidentiality and the kind of paranoia that can cause you to freeze with your idea still undeveloped. Consider the following distinctions.

- If you refuse to post details of your invention on Facebook, you're prudent.
- If you refuse to share them with an investor who wants to give you a million dollars, you're paranoid.
- If you are vague with the details when talking to the members of your networking group, you're prudent.
- If you won't e-mail about your idea because you're afraid of the message being intercepted, you're paranoid.
- If you talk to a trademark and patent lawyer about protecting your concept, you're prudent.
- If you refuse to meet with one for fear that he'll steal your idea for himself, you're paranoid.
- If you do background checks on potential employees, you're prudent.

- If you install surveillance cameras in their cubicles, you're paranoid.
- If you protect all your computers and company network with a password, you're prudent.
- If security is so elaborate that no one—not even your employees—can figure out how to get into your network, you're paranoid.

Don't let paranoia about idea piracy that will probably never happen stop you from starting your business and living your dream. Protecting your ideas is about common sense and being aware of your surroundings. But more than anything else, it's about knowing that no one can steal *you*. You are your idea. If you get inspired to run with it and make it into something brilliant, no copy will stop you.

Dreamer's Corner: A New Entrepreneur Q&A

Suzette C. Boyette, ARNP, MSN, Cofounder
www.parentseverywhere.com
sboyette@parentseverywhere.com

1. What is the name of your new business, and when did you start it?

The name of our business is Parents Everywhere, Inc., and my husband, Troy, and I started it the day after my birthday, January 9, 2007.

2. What type of business is it?

Parents Everywhere is a new media publishing company that has a network of podcasts or internet radio shows about parenting and family health. Currently, we have ten shows in our network. Our free twenty-minute podcasts are created especially for parents who want to strengthen

(continued)

family connections, to understand the latest information, or to have access to getting answers to questions. We have dedicated health-care professionals and educators who now have a voice for their passion and reach millions all over the world. Our podcasts are accessible anytime, anywhere—convenient for busy parents.

3. How has being an entrepreneur changed you?

Troy has always been an entrepreneur at heart: a big thinker with out-of-the-box ideas and the spirit of a true creator/innovator. However, I was your typical "stay-in-the-box" thinker: work for others, provide for the family, do what you are told. It was Troy's encouragement and excitement over what we could accomplish that "broke my box," and my entrepreneurial spirit was lit.

What this experience has taught me is that I enjoy being my own boss and also that I'm pretty good at it. I love the fact that I can "work" in my pajamas and no makeup and sip a cup of tea while talking to a famous author on a phone interview! I learned that I am an effective networker and a genuine steward for others' success. I also learned that I can do anything I put my mind to. It takes planning, work, and creativity, but anything can be done . . . even at 3 A.M.!

4. What is the most important lesson you have learned about starting a business?

Knowing when to turn off the "business mind" and when to turn on the "family mind." Most of us have families and other careers we are juggling while getting our businesses off the ground. It is important for us to remember why we are doing this: for our families. We want to take those incredible family vacations. We want to pay our children's college tuitions. We want to be able to give back to those we love the most. It is all out of love for our children and our spouse that drives us to make that sale or create the next product, so we can leverage our time and spend it doing what we love the most. When the children come home from school, I must be totally present in their lives as their "mommy," not as their "entrepreneur mommy."

5. Where is your business today, and what are your prospects for the future?

We started out with one podcast and only two people. Now we have ten podcasts/shows with over ten incredible people who also share our vision. We also now have over 30,000 listeners per month and are growing! We have created over 200 episodes throughout the network and are going to be adding at least three more new podcasts/shows before the end of the year. We are in the process of creating products and an ongoing online education program for parents to continue learning how to become effective parents by becoming members of Parents Everywhere. With these efforts and by collaborating with national organizations and businesses, we hope that Parents Everywhere will be a brand parents everywhere can identify with and trust.

What if the people you share your idea with will not steal it but will actually help you bring it to life?

Some people are so concerned about theft that it doesn't even occur to them that many people are likely to be inspired by their idea. But that's the reality: you are much more likely to find people who are inspired by your vision and want to help you achieve it than people who want to copy it.

So the story goes, author Jack Canfield was sitting next to Mark Victor Hansen on a plane and had been carrying around an idea for a book in his head. It was a collection of heartwarming stories that he called "Chicken Soup for the Soul." He could have kept that idea close to the vest, but instead he shared it with the gregarious Hansen, who immediately came up with great ideas for how to brand and market the books. The men became twenty-year partners and the best-selling book franchise in history was born. If Canfield had been too worried about his idea being stolen to share it with his seatmate, he might have missed out on the collaboration of a lifetime.

Human beings are inspired by original thinking; it's one of the reasons we find inventors like the Wright brothers and Thomas Edison such romantic figures. We revere people who figure out new ways to do things, and when we hear about a breathtakingly original idea for a product or company, we want to be a part of it. That's why so many young tech professionals gave up their lives for years to be in on the ground floor of internet companies during the dot-com boom of the late 1990s (okay, it was also the promise of stock options, but I digress).

You never know who is going to bring something to your new company that will send it into the stratosphere, and you never know who will give you a new twist on your vision that you had never thought of before. That's the beauty of collaboration. But it can only happen if you lay your concept out on the table and let a group of gifted people dissect, critique, and improve upon on it. Ideas are living things; they are not meant to stagnate inside your head. They need light and air to thrive. Here are some ways to reach out to others who might end up becoming critical parts of your team:

- *Make sure you can be found.* Be on Facebook and Twitter. Have a website with your name as the address. Have up-to-date business cards. You don't want to lose out on a potential life-changing collaborator because your e-mail address is out of date.
- *Talk to friends.* This is where I always begin. I have friends who would never be interested in becoming part of my company but who are priceless sources of commonsense wisdom. They know me well enough not to say, "Jen, you can't do that," because that's like waving a red flag in front of a bull. But they are full of sound advice and support. Find your most grounded, intelligent friends, and share your ideas with them. See where that takes you.

- *Talk with students.* College career groups, which you can find through career centers or online, are marvelous places to locate future employees as well as untapped reservoirs of talent. You might stumble upon gifted kids who are more than happy to energize your business in return for an opportunity to engage in something really cool right out of school.
- *Connect with entrepreneurs you already know.* People who already run companies are fantastic sources of practical resources and make wonderful devil's advocates, because they are already on the front lines and know what you're about to face.
- *Try business brainstorming groups.* Google "business brainstorming" and you'll find groups all over the country dedicated to helping their members refine their entrepreneurial innovations.

Why not have a nondisclosure agreement ready for everyone?

When you're reaching out to all these people, having a nondisclosure form, or NDA, available for all parties is just common sense. An NDA is a common document that stipulates that the signer will not reveal to any other party any information learned via a specific communication (such as a meeting) or about a specific project. Basically, it's a promise to keep a secret.

Companies of all shapes and sizes use NDAs for everything from job interviews to conference calls with potential partners because they are simple and effective. First of all, they give some basic legal cover to a company that's concerned about its ideas—even ideas that it may not end up developing—being stolen or just shared with others. If someone signs an NDA and ultimately you learn that he or she talked about your project or product with someone else who ended up copying it, you can sue that person. That's a pretty strong deterrent. Also, the mere act of signing a legal document like an NDA is enough to make most people think twice about sharing confidential information. I recommend having an NDA ready for:

- Interviewing potential employees
- Interviewing possible vendors, especially if they are manufacturers and you're developing a potentially hot new product
- Meeting with potential strategic or joint venture partners
- Meeting with advertising agencies

You don't even have to have a company yet to use an NDA. You just need to have an idea. Before you talk to anyone outside of your trusted circle of friends about it, it's not a bad idea to have them sign one. It should not be a big deal. Anyone experienced in business will understand that it's not personal. I find that having an NDA actually fosters trust, because all parties know that anything said or shared will not be circulated. In fact, NDAs are so common that some people might find it odd if you *don't* ask them to sign one.

You can find examples of NDAs for free download at Docstoc. com. You can also find all kinds of great intellectual property protection information at IPWatchdog.com.

What if you don't share your idea with anyone and it dies?

John Steinbeck said, "Ideas are like rabbits. You get a couple and learn how to handle them, and pretty soon you have a dozen." But if you don't feed your ideas, they'll die. This is another reason why it's so much more important to fear regret than to fear failure. As I said, we always lament the chances we never took and the great things we never dared to do. I can't imagine anyone at the end of his or her life has ever said, "Boy, am I glad I never started that company thirty years ago, because I'm sure someone would have snatched my idea!"

The danger in keeping your exciting business idea to yourself is that it becomes familiar, static, and stale. If you have a paradigm-shattering vision but don't do anything with it, eventually you will begin to doubt yourself. You'll begin to poke holes in it and doubt that you have the ability to turn it into a business in the first place. Ideas weren't meant to be caged; they are all free-range. The longer you keep an idea locked in your head, the mustier and more lifeless it becomes.

When you share your ideas, you energize yourself and your concept. You bring an idea to life with practical suggestions and new options. And let's say, for a second, that someone does steal your idea. If you've put yourself in a fertile, collaborative environment, you'll come up with ten other ideas that are better!

What if you're smarter than the competition?

Many individuals who have a business idea but have not made the leap seem to think there is something inherently different about the people who start companies. They assume that established business owners are somehow smarter, more educated, more street savvy, or more aggressive than they are. This misconception discourages a lot of people from launching their dreams.

But the idea that entrepreneurs are smarter or different is a myth. In fact, what if you are already smarter than the people who might steal your idea? You might be such an agile thinker that by the time they manage to copy version 1.0, you'll be at version 4.0. After all, is there any reason that someone who launches a company should be any more intelligent or creative than you? There is only one difference between someone who turns his or her vision into a going enterprise and someone who can't pull the trigger:

The motivation to act.

Motivation to act is the thing many people forget about, because they are preoccupied with their idea and everything that may get in their way. They fail to realize if they would just take action, everything that they worried about would go away naturally through momentum and execution.

While I'm at it, let's deflate some other myths about entrepreneurs.

- *Myth: Entrepreneurs have big ideas.* Not necessarily. The businesswoman who changes the world usually sets out just to change her life. Your idea can be modest and even humble, but if it's yours and you love it, then it's worth pursuing.
- *Myth: Entrepreneurs are inventors.* Hardly. Most entrepreneurs just want to put their own spin on a business model that's been around for years, like the retail storefront. In the end, it's not the invention that's your gold. It's the brand you create.
- *Myth: Entrepreneurs have a business background.* Some do. Many don't. The online company Kimbelina was started by a group of women who loved the idea of manufacturing and selling snuggly blankets and other "inspirational gifts" combined with highly personal poems, intended to bring comfort and send love. They had a passion, learned on the fly, and just did it.
- *Myth: Entrepreneurs are extroverts.* Being highly social and talkative certainly helps you meet people who can benefit your company, but it's not required. Plenty of people who are quiet and laid-back have started booming companies. However, if you are introverted I encourage you to make it of one of your goals to try to become more extroverted and/or to also have a vested partner who can be a face and voice for the brand.

In short, probably the only things entrepreneurs have in common are the will and desire to "just do it," the passion and stubbornness not to quit when things get rough, and the ability to help other people see why their creation is so wonderful.

Why not start your business working only with people you trust?

Maybe you like to talk about your ideas, but you're still nervous about piracy. In that case, rather than seek out partners you don't know but want for their skill sets, start out by sharing information with folks you already know and have worked with before. These can be friends or longtime colleagues, but the most important thing is that you feel that you don't have to worry about them. The peace of mind you get from this is amazing. You don't have to watch your back. You can trust your business—which is like trusting your baby—to people you know are motivated by more than money.

When you are planning your start-up, make a list of key people who have your complete faith, and then start having one-on-one meetings with them. Explain to them what you want to do. Ask them what they think of your idea and really listen to their feedback. Then, if they seem like a good fit, ask them if they would attend a meeting of the rest of the team when the time is right. Here are a few important tips on doing this:

- *Be careful how you ask people you trust to sign an NDA.* You do not want to insult them and possibly damage future trust. Say something like, "I trust you, but my attorney insists that everyone I talk to about the company sign one of these, so. . . ."
- *Don't just bring people on as partners because you trust them.* They should also have a useful skill set. I wouldn't hire your

pal from the eighth grade if all he knows or has been trained to do is get jelly donuts from the breakroom.

- *Make sure duties and obligations are clear.* Be sure that everyone knows his or her role and that your position as the leader is established.

Why not talk to an intellectual property attorney about trademarking or patenting your idea?

Part of being smarter than the other guy is knowing when to protect your ideas. If your idea involves an invention, you might be eligible to patent it under U.S. patent and trademark law. And if you have created a unique word, phrase, or symbol, it's possible to trademark that. Even business models have been patented, such as Amazon. com's "One-Click" purchasing idea. Patents and trademarks will protect your ideas and brand from being stolen by unscrupulous competitors.

Consulting a good patent and trademark attorney can be expensive. But even if you find out you don't need or qualify for trademark or patent protection, the consultation is time and money well spent, because you will become educated. Next Tuesday you might come up with an invention or product name that *does* demand protection. So by consulting a good attorney, you will learn about the ins and outs of what might one day be a vital aspect of your business strategy.

Lessons Learned

► It's unlikely that anyone will steal your idea, especially if the concept has yet to be proven. By the time you prove its strength, you should already have made it a brand.
► Most people think their ideas are superior to other people's, so they're not likely to want yours, or they will change yours so much it is no longer really "yours."
► Most people would rather copy than innovate.
► You can't take the visionary out of the vision.
► The unique way in which your people express your idea makes it impossible to duplicate.
► Being prudent about idea security should not cross over into paranoia.
► There are people you can trust who will help you.
► Patents, trademarks, and nondisclosure agreements are smart protection.
► If you don't share your idea with others, it will die.
► There is nothing about entrepreneurs that makes them any smarter than you.

The Next Twenty-Four

In the next twenty-four hours . . .

✓ Make a list of people you trust who might make good business allies.
✓ List the measures you can take to keep your ideas secure and secret.
✓ Download a boilerplate nondisclosure agreement.
✓ Research business brainstorming groups.
✓ Ask for referrals for an intellectual property attorney.

My Dream Plan, Part 4

List the individuals you would most love to recruit as partners, employees, or contractors in the key areas of technology, branding, sales, and customer service.

Technology:

_____

_____

_____

_____

Branding:

_____

_____

_____

_____

Sales:

_____

_____

_____

_____

Customer service:

_____

_____

_____

_____

"What if I don't have the money to start my company?"

5

In his excellent manual *The Smart Startup Guide*, business funding expert Peter Ireland pops the venture capital bubble with a simple, brutal fact: **only 1 out of 500 entrepreneurs who attempts to get some kind of venture or angel funding actually gets the money.** The other 499 waste months on business plans and pitches only to be shown the door. In my opinion, those are the lucky ones. As Ireland also points out, as soon as you accept money from an institutional investor, you could lose control of your company. It's not uncommon for eager but inexperienced entrepreneurs to sign over majority control of their companies to a venture capital firm and then, in six months or so, find themselves fired from their own companies!

The idea of venture capital funding grew to mythic proportions during the internet business bubble of the late 1990s. Suddenly, so the story went, you could come up with an outlandish dot-com business idea, put together a slick business plan, head out to Sand Hill Road in Silicon Valley, and pitch one of the major venture firms like Kleiner Perkins Caufield & Byers. Odds were not too bad that you would walk away with $50 million to launch your company, take out TV ads during the Super Bowl, and hold lavish Las Vegas parties. It was a lovely story, and largely false.

For every Google or Hotmail, there are 1,000 companies that either didn't get their money or got it, lost it all, and vanished. But even after the whole dot-com debacle, the damage was done. Entrepreneurs of all backgrounds and levels of experience started believing the Great Start-up Funding Lie:

You need venture or angel money to start a company.

This is simply not true. In fact, the belief that they must have funding from one of these sources stops many would-be entrepreneurs from ever getting started. They think, "I have to get $10 million in venture capital before I can open my doors!" But the truth is that 99 percent of start-up companies do not need venture or angel funding to launch and should not pursue it, at least not at the outset. We're going to talk about the alternatives.

The Trouble with Venture Capital

Venture capital is capital that comes from pools of investor money that venture capital firms (VCs) accumulate into funds. These companies then invest those funds in new companies that they feel have a good chance of either going public and selling stock or being bought by a larger company. Venture capital companies manage these funds and look for appropriate start-ups to fund as investments; their managers tend to enjoy celebrity status in the high-tech and start-up business worlds.

The problems with venture capital are twofold. First, it's very hard to get. VCs are looking for either existing companies with proven profits and billion-dollar growth potential or start-ups run by superstar teams. They're usually not interested in ground-floor start-ups run by novices. The second problem with VC money is that if you get it, you suddenly become accountable to people whose ultimate agenda is to get their investment and profit back as quickly as possible; your vision and passion often become secondary. Most entrepreneurs who accept VC money will give up at least 50 percent of their companies, turn over operations to an outside team, be forced to grow much faster than they might otherwise have liked, and stand a good chance of losing control of their vision completely.

I watched this painful experience firsthand when a group of my friends received a round of venture capital. Only months later, one of the cofounders was asked to leave, and the entire company almost fell apart. Once the VCs came in, they put a tremendous amount of pressure on the founders to change the way they had been doing things and to turn profits quickly. All of this changed the vision of the company and created so much internal pressure that everything exploded.

Angel investors are wealthy individuals who invest smaller sums of money—as little as $10,000 up to $1 million—in companies in return for a stake in the company. Angel investing is seen as being "friendlier" than venture capital, in part because you might deal with a single person instead of a company. But don't be fooled. We're still talking about a lot of money, and you still run the same risks. Angel investing is big business; if it weren't, there wouldn't be hundreds of angel investor clubs and groups around the country. You're going to face the same issues as VCs on a smaller scale: giving up a share of your business, possibly losing control, and maybe even being ousted.

However, the biggest problem with chasing outside investor money is the time you will waste doing it. Going after investment capital is much like gambling. You're betting the time you spend putting together your pitch on hitting the jackpot in the form of big dollars. But you would be better off spending those six or twelve months developing your ideas, networking, filing patents, creating your website, and taking orders. Many investor-backed companies start off at a disadvantage (despite their big bank balance) because while they were chasing the big dollars, some self-funded, agile entrepreneur was out there grabbing market share. The bottom line is, the more you bootstrap and build your company, the more you can prove demand so that, if and when you do need capital from VCs or Angel Investors, you will be less of a risk, and therefore have to give less away.

The Friends and Family Plan

This doesn't mean you can't raise capital through other people. You should only trust investors who have the same passion about your business idea that you do. Venture capitalists and angels often do not care about you; they care about return on investment. That's why family and friends remain one of the best, most reliable sources of start-up funding.

Even in a tough economy, there are still plenty of people with money. They may have taken it out of the stock market or real estate and now they're holding on to it, wondering what to do with it. They still want to use it. They still want to invest it. They still want it to grow. Talk to family members and friends with whom you have a trusting relationship, and tell them about your business idea. Have a written business plan ready, and explain to them clearly what you are looking for. You're not looking for an operational partner. You're after start-up capital, and if they invest, you will pay them a strong return and buy them out after a set amount of time, giving them a nice return on money that might otherwise be earning half a percent in a money market account. After all, if your father-in-law would be willing to lend you $25,000 for a down payment on a house, why wouldn't he be willing to lend that money for a business instead?

Here are some steps I suggest you take when approaching friends or family members about investing in your idea and working with them after they become investors:

- *Be direct and confident.* It may not be easy to say to a friend, "Buddy, can you spare $10,000?" Believe in your idea, and approach the discussion as a business proposal. Tell the person that you have a business opportunity and you would like to talk to him or her about investing in the business in return for a payout that exceeds what the current stock market can deliver.
- *Have a written proposal ready.* It should include a business plan, the amount of money you're seeking, the annual rate of return, and the period of time in which you will pay the investor back his or her principal.
- *Forget about what the market did in 2008 and 2009.* Its historical rate of return is 8 percent per year. You should be prepared to offer more than that to your investors.
- *Have an attorney prepare a detailed, airtight contract.* This document should lay out the amount invested, the rate of return, the payoff time, the investor's role in your company (if any), the rights of both parties, and all the other official business. Don't do any deal on a handshake, even with someone you've known for thirty years. The purpose of a contract is to protect you *and* your investors.
- *Communicate.* Keep your investors informed with regular e-mails, newsletters, or face-to-face meetings. Let them know how things are going. Be honest. If sales are slow, level with them. Keeping investors in the dark is the surest way to make them panic and take rash action.
- *Buy them out as fast as possible.* The sooner you can get third parties out of your company, the better. Even Mom and Dad should exit stage left as quickly as you can cut them a check.

Entrepreneurs Create Money

Entrepreneurs create wealth and jobs with their minds and their visions; it's what we do and who we are. If you have an idea, you can turn it into money. The relative availability of venture and angel cash in the past made some entrepreneurs lazy; why find creative ways to cut costs and raise cash when you have $15 million burning a hole in your bank account?

So I think the decline in easy investor money is a good thing for the entrepreneurial spirit. Why? Because skeptical lenders, partners, suppliers, and customers force entrepreneurs to innovate and think on our feet. We can't pick the low-hanging fruit; instead, we're forced to be smart, bold, fearless, and hyperefficient. Visit websites like YouNoodle.com, KillerStartups.com, or my own Launchers Café, and see what companies are doing to get themselves off the ground. By and large, they are not chasing after big venture dollars. They are using their own saved funds, reinvesting the dollars as they come in, trimming costs down to the bone, being creative, and doing whatever it takes to get the company rolling, produce cash flow, and stay afloat until their idea takes hold.

Raising capital is a full-time job. People underestimate how long it takes. I recommend bootstrapping as much as you can. I have a friend who is developing a skin-care product line but was laid off from her job. To avoid having to raise more capital from an outside source, she's using her skills and experience to teach at a nearby community college to earn money. You can do the same type of thing.

During my visits to the set of *The Big Idea*, I met many inspiring entrepreneurs, and we often talked about the lifestyle of bootstrapping—saving every penny, giving up even small luxuries like gourmet coffee, selling things we didn't need, and living as simply and leanly as possible. By and large, we were in complete agreement that it was the only way we wanted to grow. One of my favorite quotes about this comes from a student of Warren G. Tracy, founder and president of the Busted Knuckle Garage: "Entrepreneurship is living a few years of your life like most people won't so you can spend the rest of your life like most people can't." Any entrepreneur I know would certainly agree.

Stacy's Pita Chip Company is a perfect case in point. If you shop at Costco, you've seen the black and blue bags of Stacy's Pita Chips. Mark and Stacy Andrus started their company as a food cart in Boston's Financial District, selling all types of pita-wrapped fresh foods to ravenous Bostonians. Because a good entrepreneur wastes nothing, they took the leftover pita at the end of each day and baked it into seasoned chips, which quickly became a sensation. They made the decision to focus on snacks and rented space in a Boston pretzel bakery, creating and bagging all their pita chips by hand.

Mark and Stacy even bootstrapped their own office, renovating a 10,000-square-foot factory space and building the single cubicle out of recycled scrap wood from a shipping crate. As they moved into automated packaging and abandoned the food carts, their revenues grew to near a half-million dollars per year. They put the business in Stacy's name to qualify for Small Business Administration loans aimed at women-owned businesses, bought ancient equipment and modified it, kept staff lean by practicing "just in time" hiring, and secured several hundred thousand dollars in small business loans based on having a good business plan and existing demand, which is the key. Once you can show you have a market, it's easy to get money. By 2005, the story had a very happy ending: PepsiCo bought the then–$60 million dollar snack foods company, which continues to operate out of its Randolph, Massachusetts, offices.

Entrepreneurs create money by finding any possible way to get their ideas out in front of the public and inspiring people to buy. That way, they generate cash flow that allows them to grow their company and maybe even get funding from legitimate sources, such as small business loans, that won't take control of the business.

Dreamer's Corner: A New Entrepreneur Q&A

Millie Haynam, Founder
www.milliehaynam.com
mhaynam@yahoo.com

1. What is the name of your new business, and when did you start it?

Natural Beauty Salon and Academy, Inc., launched on November 9, 2001.

2. What type of business is it?

A salon and advanced academy for salon professionals.

3. What was the greatest obstacle you faced in starting your business, and how did you overcome it?

Getting funded. I basically kept pounding the pavement and working on deals until I got my doors open. Unfortunately salons do not have the best track record in business and are considered high-risk. I worked a deal with a landlord to give me a break on the rent if I built out the salon from the stud walls. I had my husband help me put together the place with our own two hands (well, ours and his friends' hands) and haven't looked back.

4. What has the experience of being an entrepreneur taught you about yourself, and how has it changed you?

It definitely magnifies your weaknesses. I have learned if you ignore them, they do not go away; they will find you and hurt you. I had to change my plan, be proactive in this economy to capitalize on my strengths and downplay my weaknesses. I have very little patience for laziness and ignorance, and if you've ever owned a business, you will soon see that is abundant in the workforce. I am not a good manager, so I changed my salon to booth rental so each beauty professional runs their own little business and I am just the landlord. It works so much better for me. It also gives me the freedom to pursue my other talents in writing and speaking.

5. What is the most important lesson you have learned about starting a business?

Make sure you love what you do and have a passion for it. You will be doing it a lot!

6. Where is your business today as far as earnings, size, etc.? What are your prospects for the future?

I am in a larger location but as a booth rental salon. The earnings are about the same as the first few good years, with more growth potential than ever. I have other business endeavors that I am currently working on, including a PR website for beauty professionals, a consulting business, and a writing/speaking career.

What if there are more creative ways to raise money than you realize?

There are many ways to fund your dream that will never require you to do the dog-and-pony show. You have options. Remember, you're an entrepreneur, and entrepreneurs create money! Here are some of the alternatives:

- *Fund it yourself.* Bootstrapping is the best way to launch your company—even better than getting small loans from friends or family. This is why elsewhere in this book I have recommended saving your money for a few months or moonlighting. That money can become your start-up capital. During the massive layoffs of 2008 and 2009, I saw thousands of entrepreneurs using their severance checks to fund their new companies. The following are some bootstrapping suggestions.
  - Figure out how much cash you have available to you right now, including current savings, retirement savings, incoming pay from your job, and possible severance. Should you

WHAT IF? & WHY NOT?

tap your 401(k) to launch your company, given the interest and penalties? That's up to you. But if you are under forty, it's worth discussing with your tax advisor.

○ Figure out how much your business will cost to run for the first six months. Your base must-have costs should be as low as possible: business cards, a website, a dedicated cell phone, bookkeeping services, software, and a business license are the essentials. I give a complete list of the start-up must-haves in Chapter 1.

○ Calculate how much you will need to cover living expenses and business expenses for six months, and compare that to your available cash. How much more do you need?

○ Figure out how much revenue you could realistically generate within three months if you launched your business today. For example, let's say you need $35,000 over six months to cover all living and business costs, and you have $15,000 in savings. You need $20,000 more, right? Not if your business can generate $5,000 a month in gross sales after three months. Multiply that $5,000 by three months and you have an extra $15,000 to cover start-up costs. You may only need to save an extra $5,000 (though it's usually better to save a little more, just in case; see Chapter 9).

• *Peer-to-peer lending websites.* Peer-to-peer lending is an alternative to traditional bank and personal lending and is used all over the world. Peer-to-peer lending sites connect lenders and borrowers through an online network. They allow creative investors to locate equally creative entrepreneurs whose ideas appeal to them personally and get greater potential rates of return than they would get from banks or the securities market. You get funding at reasonable terms while avoiding the bureaucracy and fees of banks. Some of the best peer-to-peer lending networks include:

○ CommunityLend.com

- ○ Globefunder.com
- ○ LendingClub.com
- ○ Loanback.com
- ○ Loanio.com
- ○ Prosper.com
- ○ VirginMoneyUS.com (courtesy of the entrepreneur's entrepreneur, Sir Richard Branson)
- *Small Business Administration loans.* SBA loans are one of the oldest ways of getting business funding, but there are some common misconceptions about them. First, when you get an SBA loan, you aren't borrowing money from the government. You're actually borrowing from a bank that's chartered by the government to make SBA loans. The government is merely guaranteeing the loan, meaning the government will repay the money if you default.

  SBA loans are not typically for companies that are just starting. Since you're borrowing from a private, for-profit bank, you need to prove you can pay back your SBA loan. Your business must already be operating so you can prove you have a solid business model and cash flow before you will be able to get a loan. Some banks will even ask for equity in your company in return for lending you money! *Never* give away part of your company for a loan.
- *Grants.* There are billions in grant dollars out there for the taking, even in hard economic times. In addition to the government grants available to women and minorities, colleges, research institutions, and hospitals sometimes offer small grants. Small is all you may need if your idea comes with a low start-up cost. Many states have business development programs that offer grants to small companies. Some of the best places to get information about grant money are business.gov/finance/financing, sbinformation.about.com, and SmallBusinessGrantsMoney.com.

- *Sponsorships.* My friend Carissa owns a company called Silver Lining. While her company was young she realized she needed capital infusion quickly and got creative. Her business consults and educates entrepreneurs, so she decided she would leverage her speaking platform to create a small business tour. She went to large companies and asked them to sponsor the tour, six came on board, and *voilà!* She acquired the capital infusion that she needed.

- *Joint ventures.* I believe joint ventures are going to be a bigger business trend in the future than they have been in the past, and entrepreneurs have the opportunity to drive the trend. If you have an idea but other companies already have the infrastructure and resources to bring the idea to life more quickly, you may want to consider teaming up with them for a joint venture. For example, there is a new bike share company currently launching in the U.S. called B-Cycle. B-Cycle was an entrepreneurial idea that was created by bringing three companies together: Humana, Crispin Porter + Bogusky, and Trek. Humana is the healthcare component, CP+B is the advertising marketing arm, and Trek is the product development arm. So instead of someone trying to make this company happen from scratch it was orchestrated in a way that leveraged three powerful existing companies that already had the resources needed to expedite its creation.

  I know several entrepreneurs who have also taken their ideas and created divisions within existing companies. With this approach the capital came from the company and they were able to instantly leverage the infrastructure and brands they were partnering with.

Opening your mind to these types of opportunities can really broaden your scope in starting your new company.

What if there are a hundred ways to start your business for a lot less than you think?

As David Bach, best-selling author of *The Automatic Millionaire* and *Fight for Your Money*, says, it's not that we don't earn enough; it's that we spend too much. Use every possible means to reduce your start-up costs. Think of yourself as being a backpacker setting off on the 2,175-mile-long Appalachian Trail. You're going to cut every ounce possible from your pack, because you've got to haul every one of those ounces up and down each hill. Similarly, you must become a merciless cost cutter. The less you spend each day in your company's operations, the more profit you'll make, the more that profit will sustain your company without outside funding, and the less you'll be obligated to a lender. Here are a few cost-cutting ideas:

- *Office space.* Work out of your home. If you need to work with a team, have each person work from home or any other space available to them, and collaborate via a free online environment like Vyew.com, Yakkle.com, Yugma.com, or Mikogo.com. Using these will not only save you rent money, but you may also be able to deduct some of the cost of your rent, utilities, and other housing expenses from your taxes.
- *Printed materials.* Companies like VistaPrint.com provide digital printing services for a very low fee, and they offer business cards, brochures, and other typical materials. Programs like Adobe InDesign and Apple's Pages make it very easy to design attractive brochures.
- *Staff.* Don't hire anyone immediately. If you can't do everything yourself, including sales, at the start, you're probably trying to do too much. Remember you can always bring on interns or hire people for sweat equity.

- *Technology*. You must have internet access and a website. That's all there is to it. For everything else, you can go cheap. If you already have a computer at home, make it work for you even if it's an older one.

- *Marketing.* Initially, your only marketing should be your website, your business card, your in-person networking, and your Facebook and Twitter pages. You don't need to spend money on anything else. Don't take out Yellow Pages ads. Don't buy listings in online directories. Word of mouth is everything; get out and meet people and create it.

- *Manufacturing*. Service businesses tend to be cheap to launch, but selling a product means that you have to manufacture it. If you're in that position, talk to a local factory or fabricator about using their equipment during off-hours, when it's otherwise sitting idle. If it's at all possible, try to make your products yourself by hand in the beginning. If you have a fantastic idea for something but don't know how to make it, learn. You are the only one you can trust to manufacture your product the right way.

- *Legal help*. Affording an attorney at the outset is probably out of the question. You can find basic legal documents for needs like incorporation, trademarks, and patents at websites like LegalZoom.com, Nolo.com, LegalDocs.com, and LegalHelper. net. It's also worth reviewing these sites and social networks like Launchers Café to get general advice on how to handle legal matters, though this is never a substitute for counsel from a licensed attorney.

- *Insurance*. If you're working for yourself, this is an unavoidable cost, and it can be expensive. Buying your own coverage, even if you're a single person, will cost $200 a month or more, even if you're willing to carry a deductible as high as $5,000. You may want to continue working part time at your job to keep getting some kind of insurance coverage, at least in the beginning.

What if

someone loved your vision enough to fund it outright?

This seems unlikely, doesn't it? But what if someone was so blown away by your idea that he or she decided to fund it with no strings attached, or with such minor strings (such as zero interest) that you couldn't resist?

It's possible from someone who knows and cares about you—a family member, friend, or mentor. Consider this scenario: You have a spouse and two children. According to U.S. tax law, a direct relative such as a grandparent can give a tax-free gift of up to $11,000 per year each to you, your spouse, and your children. That's $44,000 that would go a long way in starting up a business while reducing the giver's tax burden. You develop a pitch, call Aunt Phyllis, and tell her about your idea. She loves it, and then you ask her about making a tax-free gift so that you can fund the company without having to worry about paying off a loan. If you're lucky, she agrees. Voilà! You have some substantial start-up cash that will last a while if you're frugal.

Then there is the no-nonsense approach taken by Mark Cuban, founder of Broadcast.com and owner of the Dallas Mavericks. Mark is one of my favorite entrepreneurs because of his sheer guts and passion for innovation. For instance, in 2001, at a time when he could have kicked back with his fortune and enjoyed being an NBA owner, he founded HDNet, which operates two 24/7 high-definition television channels. In February 2009, Mark proposed a concept called "open source funding" and described his "take it or leave it" terms on his blog, blogmaverick.com:

I will invest money in businesses presented here on this blog. No minimum, no maximum, but a very specific set of rules. Here they are:

1. It can be an existing business or a start up.
2. It cannot be a business that generates any revenue from advertising. Why? Because I want this to be a business where you sell something and get paid for it. That's the only way to get and stay profitable in such a short period of time.
3. It MUST BE CASH FLOW BREAK EVEN within 60 days.
4. It must be profitable within 90 days.
5. Funding will be on a monthly basis. If you don't make your numbers, the funding stops.
6. You must demonstrate as part of your plan that you sell your product or service for more than what it costs you to produce, fully encumbered.
7. Everyone must work. The organization is completely flat. There are no employees reporting to managers. There is the founder/owners and everyone else.
8. You must post your business plan here, or you can post it on slideshare.com, scribd.com, or Google Docs, all completely public for anyone to see and/or download.
9. I make no promises that if your business is profitable, that I will invest more money. Once you get the initial funding you are on your own.
10. I will make no promises that I will be available to offer help. If I want to, I will. If not, I won't.
11. If you do get money, it goes into a bank that I specify, and I have the ability to watch the funds flow and the opportunity to require that I cosign any outflows.
12. In your business plan, make sure to specify how much equity I will receive or how I will get a return on my money.
13. No multi-level marketing programs.

That's tough-love funding from one of our era's greatest entrepreneurs. Not the type of relationship that every new business owner would tolerate, I'll grant you, but it's sure a way to stick to your efficient operational strategy. When you blend that kind of discipline and accountability with a brilliant concept and a sound business model, it's the closest thing to guaranteed success.

Why not just start your business and create cash flow?

When you can show that you can create and sustain a business, build a brand, and generate cash flow, it becomes far easier to borrow capital, find investors, and get people at major corporations to pick up the phone. If you can launch a business with a low cost base that produces a healthy cash flow right away, it will pay for itself, and you may never need to seek any sort of additional funding. Even if you do need investor capital, you will usually be asked to give up a smaller share of your ownership in the company because you have proven the model has staying power, thus reducing the risk to your investors.

Are there such businesses? You bet there are. Many service businesses are low-cost and high-return. Consulting, graphic design, freelance writing, image consulting, Web development, house staging—these are just a few of the services for which you can charge $100 an hour or more yet open your doors with a business card and a website. Other businesses are more costly, requiring either professional certification (realtor, massage therapist) or expensive equipment (production company). But even if your dream business involves manufacturing a product, which can have a very high start-up cost for design, manufacturing, and distribution, there are ways to start things rolling at a low cost.

For example, let's say that you have an idea for a new kind of board game for adults. You don't have the money to put into manufacturing or distribution, and you don't want to chase funding. What do you do? You get creative, like an entrepreneur should. You use your small start-up budget to create an online prototype of your game, and then promote it through networking and media coverage. When people come to the game website, they can play it for free for thirty days, and then they have to pay a monthly fee. After a year, you might have 1,000 people paying a small monthly fee, like $7, to play your game. That's $7,000 a month or $84,000 a year in revenue with a tiny overhead. That's money you can use, even as the online version of your game grows, to start developing the real-world version and creating a thriving brand.

Why not license your idea to a larger company?

Licensing early on is a fantastic way to build a wonderful brand with minimal cost. Licensing is an agreement granting permission to another company to make use of the intellectual property rights to your idea or your brand. Basically, you get paid for your intellectual property, and another company shoulders the cost of producing products based on it. It's one of the most important strategies for building a thriving business. Hannah Montana toys and lunch boxes, Monopoly slot machines in Las Vegas, and Ford hybrid vehicles are all great examples of successful licensing.

Licensing works because many big corporations have manufacturing facilities, infrastructure, marketing power, and money, but they lack innovative ideas and appealing brands. That's where you, the entrepreneur, come in. If you start your company and immediately begin building "brand equity" (the awareness, prestige, and emotional affinity that make a brand desirable—think Prada, Armani, and Chanel) there's a good chance that companies will want to license your idea and create products based on it. Why? Because a strong brand breeds customer loyalty and can turn buyers into devoted evangelists—an unpaid, 100 percent authentic, and totally committed sales force. That's something a company can't just manufacture, so they're better off leveraging your brand.

Your goal should be to build a brand with enough equity that licensors will share the risk with you to be a part of it. I discuss the art of building brand equity at much greater length in Chapter 7.

Licensing is a wonderful way to grow a brand and business without a ton of capital. You take advantage of your licensee's infrastructure, sales force, and relationships, and in return, they get to make sales and enjoy a kind of reflected glory from your brand. It's a way to grow your company while alleviating a lot of the operational stresses, such as managing employees and raising cash. With the Butler Bag, my goal was to have a licensing deal within two years. During that time, I needed to get so much press that it was undeniable that I had a powerful brand. After two years, I had such a track record and such great sales that I proved that the brand was desirable.

When you have reached that plateau, go to a company that is in the business of acquiring brands, and negotiate a deal. I hired a company that specializes in creating licensing deals to handle this process, because that wasn't my area of expertise. By using them, I was able to get a much better deal than if I had negotiated it myself. So my licensing partner uses the name and the technology of the Butler Bag, and I decide what tiers of distribution they will have. Someone else takes on the risk and cost. I get a capital infusion into my business and a huge new market for my brand.

Why not start an investment cooperative with family and friends?

One of the best ways to leverage friends and family in funding a new business is to start a cooperative in which everyone invests a small amount and becomes a shareholder. Typically, co-ops are founded by the people who are also their customers, which was how Honest Tea Company got their start-up capital, but there is nothing preventing you from instead making each investor a small shareholder and paying dividends each year. This way, rather than trying to get $7,500 in basic start-up cash from a single family member, you might be able to get $1,500 each from five family members and make each one a shareholder in your company. You'll want to talk to an attorney in your state about the specifics of setting something up like this, but it's a great way to spread around investor risk while lowering the barrier to investing. Let's face it: it's a lot easier to part with $1,500 than $15,000.

Entrepreneurs should keep the lines of communication open at all times. Convene a meeting of the board once a month to bring everyone up to speed on what the company is doing, answer questions, and keep everyone feeling comfortable and confident. However, make sure you have a "sunset clause" in the partnership agreement. That's a set date when the partnership expires and all investors must be paid back their principal together with any agreed-upon earnings. You don't want to scare off any potential future buyers or licensing partners by having a bunch of family members permanently attached to your company. Preselect the date when the co-op dissolves so that at that time you can pay everyone back and be free and clear to continue growing your business.

Lessons Learned

- ► Less than 1 percent of the companies that go for venture capital actually get it.
- ► Venture capital deals can cost you control of your company and a lot of time you could be spending growing it.
- ► Angel investors often want the same control as larger VCs.

- ► Bootstrapping is the best and most common way to get a business started.
- ► Friends and family are another great way to fund your start-up.
- ► Entrepreneurs and their ideas create money.
- ► There are many creative ways to capitalize your business: social lending, SBA loans, grants, partnerships, and licensing.
- ► Cash flow is king. If you can get started and generate cash, you can do virtually anything.
- ► There are many ways to reduce start-up costs if you're creative.
- ► There are always partners who will collaborate with you if your idea is strong enough.

The Next Twenty-Four

In the next twenty-four hours . . .

- ✓ List the assets you have available to you today and in three months.
- ✓ Calculate how much your business could realistically be earning in ninety days if you launched it tomorrow.
- ✓ Figure out how much more you need to save to have enough cash on hand to cover six months of personal and business expenses.
- ✓ Make a list of potential companies that might collaborate with you.
- ✓ Make a list of the friends and family from whom you might be able to get loans or tax-free gifts.

My Dream Plan, Part 5

Detail your possible funding sources, including personal savings.

Amount I have saved currently:

_____

_____

_____

Amount I could save from income in three months:

_____

_____

_____

Amount I could borrow from friends and family:

_____

_____

_____

Amount my company could bring in after three months:

_____

_____

_____

Amount my company could bring in over ninety days if I run it part time:

_____

_____

_____

_____

Total possible available capital in six months:

_____

_____

_____

_____

"What if I don't know anything about the industry I want to be in?"

6

When I first told people what I wanted to do with the Butler Bag, what I heard most often was, "Jen, you can't do it that way." From product design to distribution channels to price points, I was told that the way I wanted to do things wasn't the way they were done. I wanted to license my brand right out of the gate. My plan was contrary to conventional wisdom, people said. And so on. A lot of people wouldn't make low-cost lines because their egos said, "I'm strictly high-end." Well, as a high-end brand, when the market calls for a low-cost line, you give the market what it's screaming for. I have heard of designers and companies that never set up online distribution. Online distribution has been my lifeblood. I went against the grain by never having a storefront or a flagship store. Most people who learned about those policies told me I would doom my company because of them.

I'm still here, in part because I didn't listen. My saving grace was a combination of stubbornness and conviction that my way would work just as well or better than the way business "had always been done." Things have worked out the way I had hoped, but here's the thing: if I had known more about how the fashion accessories business was "supposed" to work, I might not have been able to think outside my particular box. The Butler Bag might never have come about, and if it had, it would have probably been a tiny niche product instead of one of the fastest-growing lifestyle brands in the country.

The truth is that ignorance of the traditional ways an industry works can be bliss if you hope to make a splash with a new business. The reason is that when you are trying to break into a competitive market, the shortest path to success is to do something shockingly original. The new only happens when someone says, "Screw the rules" and tries something that hasn't been tried before. Google has become an internet powerhouse in part because its executives had a different vision for selling online advertising. The traditional way was to have salespeople calling advertisers, but Google came up with the AdWords instant auction system. Naysayers said it wouldn't work, but then they always say that. AdWords has turned Google into a multibillion-dollar giant and changed online advertising, because the company wasn't limited by preconceived notions of how it was supposed to operate.

Don't Be Intimidated

I'm not suggesting that being ignorant about the basics of the business you're entering is a good thing. If you are trying to launch an Indonesian furnishings import-export company, for instance, you'd better know something about import-export laws, Indonesian manufacturers, how to distinguish quality handmade furniture from mass-produced junk, and so on. But when it comes to your *business model*, sometimes it pays to know as little as possible. There are as many different business models as there are people; what didn't work for someone else might be a home run for you. You could come up with an unconventional model that is a game changer. The model can be just as important as the product or service.

The trouble is that the opinions of experienced businesspeople can be intimidating. When someone who has been in your industry for twenty years tells you all the things you *must* do and all the things that *never* work, you're riveted. You take it as gospel. After all, this person has been in the business since you were in high school. He or she must know something you don't, right?

That depends. Here's my policy for judging how seriously to take someone's advice: **how successful and happy has his approach made him?** If a businessperson sits you down for "the talk," find out first how he has done in business. Is his business still successful and growing? Is he doing well financially? Does he love what he does and seem fulfilled? If the answers to those questions aren't all yes, then nod politely, thank him for sharing what he has learned, pick up the check, and excuse yourself.

Cultivate Your Ignorance

If you know too much about the "rules" of an industry, it can hamper your ability to be bold and creative and take risks that others would call foolish. There's a reason they call it "learning the ropes": when you learn too much about how a business is supposed to work, you can become tied up by convention. You lose the freedom to be agile and responsive and come up with novel products and solutions.

Here are some of the things that I do to keep myself from being held back by the conventional wisdom of my industry:

- *Don't treat the opinions in your industry's trade magazines as gospel.* The trades are good sources of news but can be poor sources of fresh ideas. I read the trades in the accessories business, but I also read magazines about branding and business innovation like *Inc., Fast Company*, and *Advertising Age*. Why? Because I don't want to be exposed to stale thinking. I'd rather get creative ideas from outside my niche and have my own creativity stimulated, and that's exactly what I find in reading other publications.

- *Don't go to too many trade events.* You'll find the same environment you find in the trades: a lot of talk but little original thought. There are probably some core trade shows and other events you need to attend to network, meet key players, and learn about companies that might be potential partners, but avoid the rest. If your goal is to build something extraordinary, you should spend your time around creative, daring people.
- *Don't watch your competition.* You'll be tempted to copy them. I have a partner whose job is to keep an eye on our competitors, mostly to make sure we're not victims of patent or trademark infringement. But I'm not exposed to that information, because that way I can't be "infected" by it. Like a student taking an exam in school, I keep my eyes on my own paper and don't worry about what others are doing.

When you avoid getting tunnel vision by allowing your thinking to be limited by industry convention, there's no limit to what you can do. For example, Tony Hsieh, CEO of the shoe company Zappos, was on Fox's *Strategy Room*, and viewers kept e-mailing to ask questions about shoes or the shoe industry. Finally, Tony said, "You know, I don't know anything about shoes. What I do know about is creating a business model." Tony built a winning company by focusing on the brand and letting the shoemakers make his shoes. Score one for him: in mid-2009, Amazon.com bought Zappos for between $850 and $928 million.

Become an Information Junkie

Creative flashes can be inspired by anything. That's why it is so important to expose yourself to people and ideas that are completely unrelated to the business you're in. Inspiration is everywhere; you just need to keep your eyes open for it. Here are some ideas for opening your mind (and eyes):

- *Go to technology events.* Be sure to attend the ones involving internet businesses. Some of the most creative ideas are coming from the online world.
- *Get to know the world of branding and marketing.* Attend professional branding and marketing events. Read the trades like *Adweek, Brandweek,* and *Advertising Age.* You'll learn about the hottest ideas in brand marketing and development from the experts.
- *Read trade magazines from industries unrelated to yours.* I've gotten business ideas from the music industry, the auto industry, and others but rarely from the fashion or accessories industry.
- *Interview movers and shakers.* Ask key players from unrelated businesses to lunch and query them on how they do things. Invite them to critique your business model from their own perspective. You might shake something loose that will help you solve a problem or prevent one.

Become an information junkie; I certainly am. I'm constantly on a quest for knowledge. Every day at 9 A.M., I get *Advertising Age, Daily Beast,* and Mediabistro.com e-mails, and they are treasure troves of information. When you're traveling by train or plane, go to the newsstand before departure and grab a couple of magazines to read. What you learn in one segment of business can always be applied to another. It doesn't matter what businesses they are. Don't just read what you're familiar with.

I also attend the events that people I want to learn from attend. There are a lot of times in the evening when I don't feel like going to events or reading all these e-mails, but I attend the events and read the information anyway, because I know I'm going to come away with something valuable and stimulating. Before I ever invest my time, I make sure I'm keeping my eyes open for opportunity.

Think Like a Kid

The key to making all this work is not to artificially restrict your thought process. For example, my daughter the other day said to me, "Mommy, I really don't like carrying an umbrella. Why can't you make a jacket that has an umbrella in the hood, so you just push a button and it pops up when I need it?" I thought about that for a second and said, "You know what? You're right!" I don't know how to execute that idea yet, but there is probably a way to do it.

My kids do not have boundaries. Most kids don't. Every kid is a born entrepreneur. They are born to do what I call "thinking around corners." They don't come with preconceptions about what's possible and what's not. They are completely open to everything, because they lack the filter that makes most adults worry about being embarrassed or sounding foolish when they propose wild ideas or question the way of things. Being a child is about being open to opportunity, observing and absorbing everything, and coming to your own conclusions. Being an entrepreneur is about the same thing. Some of my greatest ideas and inspirations have come from watching what my children think and do. Children see things not as they are but as they can be. By watching them, I am learning to think around corners myself.

If you want to be an entrepreneur, spend time with kids. If you don't have some of your own, watch a friend's or relative's kids in action. Observe how they think. Get into the kid mind-set in which you question everything. It becomes natural. Many of us accept the way things are and become complacent. We have to retrain our brains. Maybe that should become part of your business protocol each week: talking to kids and listening to the questions they ask.

For instance, not long ago my daughter, who was four at the time, suddenly asked me, "Why is the sun always full but the moon changes?" Those are the types of questions that lead to discoveries—questions that can change the world. When you free yourself from knowledge that restricts your mind, you can think in ways that overturn business models, spawn new markets, and change the competitive balance in your industry.

The Mindful Entrepreneur

One of my mantras is "Don't judge; be inspired." Judgment is part of human nature. But instead, it makes more sense to stop and be mindful of the way something works or is built and ask, "Why is it this way? Does it have to be?" Mindfulness comes when you just observe things in the moment. It's an awesomely powerful tool. I try to practice mindfulness every day—stepping out of the flow of what I'm doing for a brief time and just being in the moment, appreciating what's going on around me. When you can do that, you see in a new way. Mindfulness creates fertile ground for inspiration. You become inspired to change things.

How many products, companies, and industries have started because someone had the audacity to say, "Can't we do this differently?" Go to a great website like Bootstrapper.com, a blog community for entrepreneurial types. You'll find a bunch of daring, around-the-corner thinkers.

Yvon Chouinard, founder of Patagonia, is a great example. Today, he runs a $300 million clothing company that's renowned for shutting down on days when the surf is up so its employees can hit the waves. But a few years back, the company was stagnant. What did Chouinard do? He focused on values, taking a bunch of employees to a retreat in Argentina to figure out how they could remake the company. What came out of that was the company's famous focus on combining work and play, a balance that inspired everyone in the company to work and play harder. That bold direction revitalized Patagonia.

When you're inspired, everything becomes possible. That is a beautiful state of mind to be in. If you're not inspired, I can think of three possible reasons why:

- You're not doing what you really love to do.
- You are doing what you love, but you're not making an effort to be mindful.
- You're over-multitasking.

I'm a big fan of multitasking. After all, I'm the woman who sits in front of the TV watching the news and technology shows with her laptop and updates her Facebook and Twitter pages while answering important e-mails. But you have to use it in moderation. Ask yourself what is the best use of your time, delegate some of the details, and give yourself some time each day to be mindful. Stop moving and see how things work. Do thought experiments. Let your mind wander, and let inspiration find you. When you're in the moment, you free your mind to ask disruptive, "What if we did it *this way*?" types of questions that can transform your business and give you a powerful competitive edge.

I'll Stop Procrastinating Tomorrow

Finally, don't use lack of knowledge as a reason to procrastinate in starting your company. Forward motion is everything; once you start, good things will happen. But would-be entrepreneurs take classes, read books, and attend trade shows instead of launching their companies. They tell themselves little white lies like, "After I take that class, I'll start my company," or, "As soon as I feel like I know enough about distribution, I'll open my store."

You will never know enough about your business to feel 100 percent comfortable starting it. Launching a company, quitting your job, and putting your neck on the chopping block is a fundamentally uncomfortable thing. If you wait until you have enough knowledge that you feel comfortable launching your business, you'll never do it. Accept that you are taking a step far outside your comfort zone and that initially you are going to have moments of panic. You can handle them.

Dreamer's Corner: A New Entrepreneur Q&A

Cathy Gregg, Founder
www.cautionunlimited.com
cgregg05@gmail.com

1. What is the name of your new business, and when did you start it?

My company is Caution Unlimited, LLC, and I started it in July 2007 in Scottsdale, Arizona.

2. What type of business is it?

Self-defense instruction and consulting, and Taser sales. I focus mainly on women's self-defense but also do corporate training and seniors. I do a cane defense class with the seniors; it's really interesting.

3. What was the greatest obstacle you faced in starting your business, and how did you overcome it?

My greatest obstacle was actually myself. I came from a long corporate management background, and I started everything myself without being able to delegate to anyone. I had to learn to outsource things that aren't my forte. You need a team to run a business; everything can't possibly be done by one person . . . at least not well.

4. What has the experience of being an entrepreneur taught you about yourself, and how has it changed you?

I was formerly the president of a manufacturing company and now have a service and retail company. The learning curve has been tremendous, but I learned that I can really do (or learn) anything that I set out to do. I'm a hyper, type-A personality, and it has actually taught me to slow down and become more detail oriented. I have also added many new friends to my circle as a result of outsourcing and letting other people help.

(continued)

5. What is the most important lesson you have learned about starting a business?

I have learned so many things about various parts of my business (marketing, development, recruiting, accounting) that I always took for granted before because I always had staff to turn to. But now I have to learn everything for myself, even if I outsource it, and I have to study it first to make a sound business decision.

6. Where is your business today as far as earnings, size, etc.? What are your prospects for the future?

I am taking the women's self-defense portion of my business national and just hired my first two trainers. I am planning on hiring a minimum of ten trainers per year in all states.

What if you know more than you think?

We tend to pick up information about topics we care about. So if you've spent years interested in the making of natural soaps and cosmetics, even if you haven't actually made any yourself, it's likely that you already know more about the business than you realize. In fact, I'll bet you know enough today to start a business as long as you "hit the ground learning" along the way!

Do a knowledge audit. Make a list labeled "What I Know." Under that heading, write down everything you already know about your business—from how products are made to how they are priced, who the market leaders are, your main competitors, and so on. Then make another list labeled "What I Think I Know." Under that heading, write down what you're pretty sure about, which can be anything from the laws that apply to your industry to the best companies to hire to handle your sales. When you're done, take stock of both lists. I'll bet you'll be shocked at how much knowledge you already have.

I have seen this scenario play out with new entrepreneurs more times than I can count. They realize that the barrier to entry for a new business isn't really as high as it seems from the outside, because there are only a few essential pieces of knowledge you have to have to make a business fly at the outset. They are:

- What your brand is about
- The market for your idea and what the people in that market care about
- How you will communicate the value of your idea to those people
- How much it will cost to deliver what you're selling and how much you can sell it for

There's nothing in that list about understanding distribution channels, just-in-time manufacturing, or how to not get taken to the cleaners when leasing commercial space. That's because those things are not essential to getting started. Getting started is *everything*. Once you create momentum behind your company, you will start to attract knowledge and people like a magnet. You'll learn by doing, because you have no choice.

What if not knowing the rules means you can make your own?

When Starbucks began its nationwide expansion back in 1987, its leaders did everything "wrong." They charged three times as much as competing chains for what everyone agreed was a commodity that could be bought anywhere and should be priced accordingly. They opened multiple stores on the same block in some major cities like New York and Boston, competing against themselves. They retained corporate ownership of each store when everyone "knew" that the only way to expand was to franchise. They made numerous other strategic "mistakes."

Guess who was right. I think global expansion, more than 16,000 coffee houses at its peak, and a major cultural impact on music, books, and film give Starbucks the right to gloat. You know you've hit the big time when the Simpsons make fun of you. Not being bound by some set of unspoken rules let Starbucks create its own playing field instead of playing on someone else's, and it can do the same for you.

Instead of climbing over the walls built by your rivals, you can tunnel under and change the game. Netflix took on Blockbuster not by going head-to-head with the company but by going around it—creating its own movie recommendation software that has revolutionized how we choose the movies we watch at home. The company has shipped more than two *billion* DVDs and Blu-ray discs to its customers, and because it patented its business model, it was able to sue Blockbuster for infringement when the onetime rival started its own online video subscription service. Here's what I've taken from Starbucks, Netflix, and others about making your own rules:

- *Be aggressive.* Go against the grain of your industry. IBM did this back in the 1990s. Its strategists realized that the personal computer they had pioneered was being made cheaper and better by other companies, and those companies were eating their lunch. They had the vision and guts to reinvent themselves as a services company.
- *Plug your ears.* As I said previously, as soon as you announce your plans, you'll be subjected to a chorus of know-it-alls telling you that what you want to do can't be done. Refuse to take their calls. Delete their e-mails. Avoid them at

restaurants. Go into "entrepreneurial quarantine" so that your vision isn't tainted or turned aside by the fears of others. Surround yourself with colleagues who thrive on outlandish new ideas and give constructive feedback and keep going.

- *Don't telegraph your punches.* Sharing your ideas is beneficial, but once you have a sales and marketing strategy in place, keep the specifics to yourself. Keep your head down and go into "quiet mode." This helps you deliver a "shock and awe" uppercut to the marketplace when you roll out your strategy. Plus, the media loves to cover the new and daring. If you appear to come out of nowhere to make a big splash, you stand a good chance of landing coverage that will enhance your brand.

- *Be relentless.* Once you have a strategy that you believe in, choose a timeframe such as one year to implement it, and during that period, stick with your strategy no matter how discouraging the results. Aggressive, original ideas take time to catch on. If your launch period runs out and your strategy still isn't yielding big results, then it's probably time to rethink and regroup.

- *Think at least three steps ahead.* If your gutsy business model is a success, someone will be at work trying to "hack" or reverse engineer a copy. But if you are always several jumps ahead of the other guys, you won't ever have to worry about being co-opted. When your first product rolls out, be thinking about versions 2.0 and 3.0. Always do what is unexpected, and do it first. That's how I've kept my brand fresh and in the public eye.

What if your other experience is relevant in your new industry?

So you've spent fifteen years working as a teacher, and now you think you would like to launch your own company helping parents use the internet to create their own custom storybooks for their children. Great idea. "But," you say to yourself as you lie in bed at night, "I don't know anything about running a business."

So what? Teaching is about communicating with kids and their parents, right? And what is creating storybooks about? The same thing. Chances are you know what stories and pictures make kids smile. You know what their parents want to teach them, and you know how to connect with kids as well as Mom and Dad. You know your market. You also know how school districts operate, which is perfect, because you probably want to market your service through schools to reach as many parents as possible.

See what I mean? There are plenty of areas of practical experience that can be invaluable no matter what kind of business you want to launch—knowledge that's referred to as "transferable." We all have transferable knowledge and skills accumulated from previous experiences:

- Accounting and bookkeeping
- Sales
- Marketing
- Graphic design
- Purchasing
- Manufacturing
- Training
- Computer programming

That's only a partial list. It's likely that no matter what past careers you've had, some of that experience can be applied to your start-up. If you've managed people, developed new products or services, taught others, or sold virtually anything, you have talents that can be called into service for a new venture. For instance, I was a professional fitness competitor in my old life. Do you think that experience has proved valuable in developing lifestyle brands for busy women who want to look their best? You bet it has!

Why not act aggressively so you'll make bigger mistakes and learn faster?

In his incredible book *Good to Great: Why Some Companies Make the Leap . . . and Others Don't*, Jim Collins writes that the enemy of most companies is not what they do badly, but what they do just well enough to get complacent. Established companies tend to be a bit fat and happy—slow to recognize a threat and even slower to respond to it. Look how slowly General Motors reacted to Toyota's new, lean manufacturing model that promised reduced cost with higher quality. They ignored it until it was too late. The company's attitude was basically, "We're GM. We'll always be on top." Except that now Toyota is dominating the U.S. market share, and GM is owned by the government.

When in doubt, act boldly, aggressively, and fearlessly. I believe in the philosophy of making loud mistakes, meaning that if you're going to act, make your actions big and brash and unexpected. You'll set complacent competitors back on their heels. You'll also automatically make some mistakes that will be the best teachers you've ever had. If I hadn't botched my initial foray into manufacturing handbags, I might not have learned the secret tricks to getting the most from contract manufacturers.

Here are some great unexpected moves:

- Just open for business and start selling.
- Patent your business model if you can.

- If you have multiple products, roll them all out at once.
- Post a video about your company and product on YouTube. Make it professional—something that can be picked up by the news media.
- Go after your main competitor in his area of greatest strength.
- Do something outrageous to get attention, such as holding a punk rock concert at your offices to announce your company's debut.
- Immediately start soliciting major players in your industry as potential partners.

The meek don't inherit the earth in business. Fortune favors the bold.

Why not find a mentor who's as unconventional as you are?

Working with a mentor is a fantastic way to learn about all aspects of business, as we have discussed. It's always worthwhile to talk with experienced professionals and find out about the lessons they have learned in the trenches. But if you're trying to remake the rules of your industry, you need a mentor who thinks the same way you do: broad and bold. In other words, you need someone who practices "creative destruction."

Creative destruction is the philosophy of tearing down old models for doing things to spark innovation. We're seeing that right now in the print newspaper business, in which the decline of the metropolitan daily paper is also sparking brainstorms in blogging, mobile news delivery, news gathering, and revenue models for the print papers that are left. People who practice creative destruction relish the chance to turn an industry upside down, and they thrive on chaos because of the opportunities it creates.

Find a mentor who fits that description, and you'll find someone who can help you build your dream. It will probably be somebody like Herb Kelleher, the spicy, wacky, and brilliant CEO of Southwest Airlines. At a time when every other airline seems to be hanging on for dear life, somehow his airline is profitable. They've done it in part with vicious cost cutting but also by being, well, weird. Flight attendants have been known to pop out of overhead bins and rap the safety instructions. Their boarding method is like hand-to-hand combat. But it all works. Find a mentor who does things his or her own way, like Herb Kelleher, and you will probably learn a great deal about how others successfully do business the "wrong way"—and some incredible secrets you can leverage to get an edge over your competition and beat the odds.

There are mentors who have made their fortunes and are now retired and dedicate their time to mentoring new talent, but many mentors are still busy running their own companies and will often charge for their time. If you feel like this person could change your life, then consider paying for their advice. Hiring a great mentor can be one of the wisest business investments you make.

Why not do an internship?

If you're concerned that you lack some essential basic knowledge of how your industry operates, consider taking an internship. They aren't just for college students anymore. They are for anyone who's trying to create opportunities in his or her field. They are also a fantastic way to learn about an industry from the inside. As economic upheaval forces many people and companies to change their plans for the future, internships for middle-aged folks and even baby boomers are becoming more common. Companies realize they can tap years of experience for little or no money. But it's a two-way street. You can use an internship to get an inside view of how things run on a daily basis. Then leave, take what you know, and apply it to your new company.

The best way to go the internship route is simply to make a list of companies you might like to intern with and then contact each one. Be direct, and tell them you're looking to learn more about the industry and would love to discuss some kind of internship arrangement. It's up to you to make that fit with your job schedule. You can also try websites like Internships.com and InternZoo.com.

If you land an internship, try to work in every aspect of the company that you can, learning as much as possible. Take notes and observe. When the time comes for the internship to end, make sure you don't sign anything with a noncompete clause or anything else that might restrict you from doing business in the same industry as the company you interned for. Finally, make connections with people at the company where you're interning who seem to share your passion for innovation and creativity. They might become partners or employees later on.

Lessons Learned

- ► Knowing too much about a business can restrict your thinking. Being a successful entrepreneur requires thinking outside the box and defying conventional wisdom, which can be easier when you don't worry about how business is "supposed to be done."
- ► Worthwhile advice will come from people who have already achieved what you want to achieve.
- ► Reading only trade publications or attending only industry events can limit your thinking. You open your mind

by exposing yourself to as many different industries as possible.

► To be truly innovative, you must learn to think like a child.

► Mindfulness helps you be in the moment, step out of the rush of your endless to-do list, look at why and how things work, and imagine alternatives.

► Procrastination is just a way to avoid potential failure.

► Bold, fearless action makes up for a great deal of inexperience.

► More of your previous experience than you realize is relevant to starting your company.

The Next Twenty-Four

In the next twenty-four hours . . .

✓ List the things you know and think you know about the industry you want to enter.

✓ List companies in your industry that you could potentially intern for.

✓ List the best trade shows, TV shows, and magazines in industries that have nothing to do with your industry.

✓ Think of three ways you could spend time around children to see how they think.

✓ Think of three things you could do to open for business in a bold, surprising, and publicity-generating way.

✓ List the five most important "rules" of your business sector, and then figure out how you can break each one.

My Dream Plan, Part 6

Detail the nature of your market.

Who is my market?

_____

_____

_____

Where is my market located?

_____

_____

_____

How will I sell to my market?

_____

_____

_____

What unmet need can I fill?

_____

_____

_____

What does my market care about most?

_____

_____

_____

_____

Who else is sellig to this market?

_____

_____

_____

_____

"What if I don't know anything about branding and marketing?"

7

We're surrounded by marketing and branding: it's in magazines, on lavish outdoor signage and billboards, and in costly television ads. For inexperienced entrepreneurs, this brand saturation can be incredibly intimidating. It suggests that to have a prayer of building a successful company, you need a master's degree in marketing and the creative genius of the people who came up with Apple's "Think Different" branding campaign. The fear of not having what it takes to create a stellar brand and an award-winning marketing plan can paralyze entrepreneurs.

It's an unnecessary fear. Simply put, a cool ad campaign, logo, and slogan do not equal a great brand. Sure, they're nice to have, but brands that win hearts and minds are more about emotional connection, authenticity, originality, and consistency than about spending big dollars with some Madison Avenue agency. There's a reason I haven't spent millions on traditional ads: that's not what my brand is built on. It's built on products that solve problems, online interaction with my customers, a constant media presence, and great visual design in everything from my products to my retail signage. You can do marketing and branding, even if you've never written a word of advertising copy. You can do this because you are your brand. Don't worry, I'll explain.

What Is a Brand?

A brand is a set of qualities attached to you, your company, your product, or your service that carries with it the implied promise that when customers come into contact with your brand, they will have a predictable, enjoyable experience. Think it's the food that has made McDonald's one of the world's most successful companies? Think again. It's the brand. When you think of the McDonald's brand, what comes to mind? How about:

- Golden arches and the yellow and red store design
- The Big Mac and other classic food items
- Ronald McDonald and the other classic characters
- Clean bathrooms
- Play areas
- A family friendly environment

When people go to a McDonald's, they know they will have the same, consistent experience whether they're in New York or Moscow. The collection of widely known qualities that carry the McDonald's promise and produce predictable emotions and responses in its customers forms the company's brand. Brands have three primary purposes:

1. Communicate the unique value the company or person offers.
2. Suggest emotionally appealing qualities that create *affinity*, a sense of ownership and membership that fosters customer loyalty.

3. Promise consistent quality or performance not only for the main brand, but for any new or licensed products under the brand's "umbrella." For example, the Virgin Group, the company founded by Sir Richard Branson, has rolled out two new airlines, Virgin America and V Australia, in the past three years. It was able to do this because the company's original airline brand, Virgin Atlantic, is so strong that it automatically lends the new airline brands a positive glow—what marketers call a "halo effect."

Brands' emotional appeal is undeniable. They are why people become such loyalists about some of the products they buy and the companies they patronize. Most of us make our buying decisions based on emotion, not logic, though we use logic to rationalize our choices later. So brands allow us to define who we are. As British economist John Kay said, "I am irresistible, I say, as I put on my designer fragrance. I am a merchant banker, I say, as I climb out of my BMW. I am a juvenile lout, I say, as I pour an extra strong lager. I am handsome, I say, as I put on my Levi jeans."

The following are some top brands and what they allow their typical loyal customer to say about themselves.

- *Harley-Davidson.* Free spirit, nonconformist, true American
- *Whole Foods.* Healthy, affluent, cares about organic agriculture
- *Prius.* Cares about the environment, progressive, thrifty
- *DeWalt tools.* Concerned with quality, professional, handy, hardworking
- *Blue Note Records.* A true jazz aficionado, sophisticated, has good taste
- *Jack Daniel's.* Uncomplicated, not a trendy drinker, appreciates simple things

As an entrepreneur, your brand is you—your passion, motivation, inspiration, and story. That's why the most important part of developing your brand is connecting with your customers in person, on Facebook, and through the media. If you have real passion about your idea, that's going to come out no matter how unpolished you might feel on camera or in front of a microphone. You are your company's best branding asset, because people are always inspired by other people who are following their dreams.

You Can Do Branding and Marketing

But when you see some of these powerhouse brands I've mentioned, it's easy to be overwhelmed. You don't have a million-dollar brand development and marketing budget and years of branding experience; how could you possibly do what these companies have done? Always remember, every brand had a beginning: no brand was ever "born" big.

You may not be able to do things on the scale the big corporations do them, but you can follow the same principles that lead to a winning brand. I did, and doing so transformed my business from an anonymous upstart to a nationally recognized lifestyle brand in just a few years.

One of the key changes you'll have to make is focusing just as much of your attention and energy on brand development as on deliverables. So many entrepreneurs focus only on their product or service. The product or service is important, of course. You have to deliver quality and value. But branding is how you create desire and demand for what you're selling. It's how you make buyers *anticipate quality and value before they have even seen your product or experienced your service.* You can have the most wonderful product in the world, but if its brand is weak and unappealing, it's going to die before anyone knows about it.

A great example is the Betamax home video recorder. When it came out in the mid-1970s, it was clearly superior to its competitor, the VHS format. But the VHS format had the better brand. It quickly became that format everyone knew about and wanted. Beta-format video is now a curiosity only used by hard-core video buffs.

Branding and marketing may not be something you know now, but they are definitely something you can learn. Successful branding and marketing is a puzzle with four pieces:

1. A research-based understanding of your market and what motivates the people in it—what they want, what they fear, what they aspire to, etc.
2. The insight to develop a brand that satisfies one or more of those core needs and wants. Often, this takes the form of a message or true story that inspired you to build your company in the first place.
3. The creativity to develop unique and compelling ways of communicating your brand to your customers from multiple directions—media, the internet, cultural events, retail, and so on.
4. The consistency and discipline to keep throwing your brand message out there repeatedly and relentlessly without constantly changing it.

Can you put those pieces together for your own business? Of course you can. You may not have a marketing background, but you know your audience. You know what emotional needs your product or service fills, and you can probably think of creative ways to connect with the people who will buy what you're selling. The last part, discipline, is simply a matter of going public, effectively communicating the right message, and sticking with it. If you can do those things, you can brand and market your company or product.

Resurrecting Brands

What is the difference between branding and marketing? Branding is everything you and your company do to support and reinforce that implied promise to the customer, from packaging and quality control to customer service and website appearance. As former Disney CEO Michael Eisner said, "A brand is a living entity, and it is enriched or undermined cumulatively over time, the product of a thousand small gestures." *Marketing*, on the other hand, is everything that communicates that brand to the public—advertising, e-mail, public relations, event sponsorships, partnerships, and more.

One of the amazing things about branding and marketing is that they can make or break a product all by themselves, regardless of its quality. Someone could be a very successful entrepreneur just by going back to failed products and reintroducing them to the market with a different brand and message. What didn't work a few years ago could be a blockbuster now; you just have to get past the "we've seen it" mind-set, and that's the purpose of a new brand: to have fresh branding strategies.

Sometimes, making a brand work is just a matter of waiting for its time to arrive. When I pitched my Leader Girlz doll idea to the chief marketing officer of a very successful toy company, he listened and then said, "Honey, do you know how many times other people have pitched this same idea and failed?" I replied, "Yes, but first of all, they weren't me. Second of all, every day is a different day, timing is different, and people are different. For example, this is the first time we've had a woman run for president. Women have actually catapulted into leadership roles because of Hillary Clinton and Nancy Pelosi. The world is different. A doll called LeaderGirlz is more than relevant today!"

My point was that my branding strategy was going to be different. My dolls are different. How I plan to launch will be different. Certainly the timing was different. You have to take all that into consideration. Did the last idea launch nationwide in major retailers? Probably not. Did it have a brand supported by a huge online presence and connections with women's and girls' groups? Probably not. Just because the general concept failed before doesn't mean it will again. If you build a fantastic brand behind an idea, ensure excellent quality and customer service, and establish a strong and continuous online and media presence, you can make an idea soar.

Channel Surfing

Once you have your story in place and your brand qualities established, treat branding and marketing like a multilayer cake; they have to happen all day every day. There should be a constant layering and re-layering of the cake—a continual pushing of your message into the marketplace. Branding and marketing are done via "channels." A channel is simply one means of getting your message out to the public. Channels include:

- Websites
- Blogging
- Social networking (Facebook, MySpace, Twitter, LinkedIn, etc.)
- E-mail marketing and e-newsletters
- TV appearances
- Radio appearances
- Newspaper and magazine coverage
- Speaking
- In-person networking
- Infomercials
- Sponsorships
- Public events
- Celebrity giveaways

That's thirteen strong channels right there, and there are more. I haven't included the ones I don't use myself, like advertising or direct mail. I've never run an ad for the Butler Bag in my career and won't unless a mind-blowing creative idea presents itself; it's too expensive and doesn't get the results I want. For other companies with monster ad budgets, such as Budweiser and AT&T, advertising may be more effective. But until you have the budget to saturate your market with ads, your money is probably better spent elsewhere.

The point is, once you have your story and brand identity in place, you need a system that constantly pushes them out to the public via as many channels as possible *every single day*. Established companies can push hardest on the channels that have worked best for them. But since you don't know what channel is going to grab people before you start, you need to work them all. Publish a column or a blog. Solicit radio and TV appearances. Contact organizations about speaking engagements. Network every chance you get. Make sure you have a strong, fresh presence on social networking sites.

You should always be working your channels and updating your message. Once you establish a strong presence in one, use it to get another one. For example, as soon as a store opens an account to sell Butler Bag products, we send that client a stand for our bags that lets them prop the bag open and put stuff in it. We also send them a stand that goes next to the bags and is designed to hold copies of articles from magazines. Whenever a new article on the Butler Bag runs in a major magazine like *O* or *People*, we send our retailers a copy. That makes it easy for them to post that article in a place where their customers can read it when they're shopping. That's the sort of thing that resonates with buyers and reinforces the brand. It gives the consumer something new to talk about and also lets us use press coverage to build retail relationships. That builds sales, which builds further press interest. Your channels should be synergistic, feeding off each other and growing one another.

Be Your Own Publicist

Many people want a publicist right out of the gate, but spending $5,000 or more a month when you're launching is almost impossible. The first thing you need to do in marketing is to learn everything you can about public relations. You need to develop press instincts and relationships with reporters, editors, producers, and program directors.

Invest in a course in media relations through a company like RTIR (RTIR.com), Media Bridge (themediabridge.com), or a local university. If tuition isn't in your budget, you can also read books like *Media Training A–Z* by T. J. Walker and Jess Todtfeld. Become your own best publicist. Learn what goes into an effective media campaign. Then you can write your own TV spots and content for magazines, and later you can actually guide your publicist. After all, you know your business and your story better than anyone else. As for marketing, read and observe. Read the major marketing and branding magazines. Deconstruct the best brands out there: Apple, Nike, Google, Starbucks, Sketchers, BMW, and Rolex. What do they have in common? Visual appeal, a strong emotional message, uniqueness, and consistency.

For example, BMW designs beautiful, high-performance luxury cars built to drive the autobahn. There is a unique BMW look: muscular yet agile. The company logo is also instantly recognizable. The emotional message is equally muscular; a BMW driver knows his car tells the world he is sophisticated and affluent and cares about quality and performance above all else. The uniqueness of the brand lies in its comparison to other luxury brands like Mercedes-Benz and Lexus. Whereas those cars are perceived as being more about luxury for its own sake, BMW is perceived as being first and foremost a high-end car for people who love to drive. Finally, the company's slogan, "The ultimate driving machine," has remained unchanged since 1976. Such consistency lets people feel confident that the brand they love has not changed, either.

Consistency is one of the most important qualities a brand can have. There are companies that change their logo, slogan, and brand identity more often than Madonna changes costumes on stage. Sometimes I think they do it just because their executives want something new. McDonald's and Coca-Cola have been two of the worst offenders, going through multiple catchphrases before arriving at their current ones, "I'm Lovin' It" and "Open Happiness," which—let's face it—are pretty lame.

When you have a strong brand story and message, stick with it. Apple hasn't changed its "apple with a bite" logo in more than twenty years. It's easy to be lured by the new, but if you have something that works, don't change it. You should always be refreshing your brand with new stories, channels, and products, but keep the fundamentals—your visual identity, slogan, personal story, and emotional message—consistent unless they don't work anymore. You'll save yourself a lot of money and headaches, and spend your time networking and speaking to the media instead of sitting in creative meetings going over logos.

Web: Not for the Do-It-Yourselfer

One area, however, where you should try to find the funds to hire a contractor is for your internet presence. The internet is the most critical branding and marketing tool for any business, and it's important to have people on your team who know how to leverage it for your benefit. There are so many vital steps any new company needs to take online: designing a website, building and maintaining an e-mail interest list, sending out regular e-mails or e-newsletters, keeping up with Facebook, Twitter, and MySpace, blogging, monitoring online media for stories and coverage opportunities, and even using online productivity tools to make your company run more smoothly. That work gets a lot easier and more profitable when you have a designated internet genius around.

One thing you'll notice about me is that I have a lot of websites: JenGroover.com, ButlerBag.com, LaunchersCafe.com, What-IfandWhyNot.com, and many more to come. This is because when I have an idea that I love, I have an internet team in place that puts up a website for it as quickly as possible. I'm not an expert in Web design or programming, but the members of my internet team are. They also maintain the written and video content of my other sites so everything is up to date. Nothing makes your brand look more out of date than a website or blog with old content.

That said, don't become obsessed with having a world-class website right out of the gate. Unless your business is internet-centric like Google, you don't need one. A good site might cost $100,000, and there are better ways to spend that kind of cash when you're just starting out. So have a site at the beginning, but keep it simple. Simplicity sells. You will have a higher conversion rate with something clean and simple. If your site is too flashy and there are too many distractions, customers might forget what they are looking for. If you simply can't pull together the money to hire a Web designer right now, you can create a simple and clean temporary site yourself using the tools you find at domain registration websites. There are hundreds, and the best ones have tools right there for you. You can get a website and shopping cart in about twenty minutes.

Once you grow and have more money, then you can upgrade to a professionally built website. Don't get swindled into thinking you have to spend tens of thousands of dollars to build a website. If you have the money, it's great, but when you're starting out, you probably don't.

You can learn more about great brands and online branding at websites like these:

- CoolHomePages.com
- BrandsoftheWorld.com

- WebDesignerDepot.com
- Brandchannel.com
- Allaboutbranding.com

Authenticity Is Everything

When Sara Blakely launched Spanx, she made sure that the whole world knew that she was frustrated with how stockings were made for women and why. The product had an origin story with a theme similar to mine: frustration with an existing product. Sara got sick of the feet of her panty hose, cut the feet out of a pair, and loved how much easier they were to put on and how much more comfortable they were. She went to manufacturers with the idea, and they all told her it wasn't a good one. One person picked up on it, and now it's a $100 million-plus company. That should be a familiar pattern to you by now.

That story became part of the Spanx brand. People connected with the American dream aspect of it: young woman has brilliant idea, perseveres against long odds, and becomes a mogul. With a great brand, you sell the story first. The product becomes a way someone can "own" a piece of a story they admire. You are selling the association that consumers have with the brand. As you're preparing to create and market your brand, figure out what your story is. It doesn't have to be dramatic, just authentic. Did you come up with your idea based on something that happened in your childhood? Were you inspired by one of your kids? Did a grandparent own a store and encourage you to own your own business one day? Stories connect us as human beings, and your brand story can be a powerful tool for growing your company, as long as it is 100 percent authentic.

Even if you get all the right messages and people in place, your brand and company will only succeed in the long run if you *keep it real*. In other words, everything about what you do and what you sell should reflect the inspiration, passion, and values that got you started in the first place. We live in a marketing-saturated society and, especially in the wake of the economic collapse of 2008 and 2009, Americans are sick of shallow, phony messages. We're in a new era of craving what's real. Social networking is a profound example of that, because it allows real people to connect in real time without any filtering. Tony Hsieh of Zappos, who I talked about earlier, is a wonderful example of someone who uses social media to create transparency and authenticity. In person, he is not the most outgoing guy, but through his constant presence on Facebook and Twitter, he connects with people so that they feel like they know and support him and his company.

The popularity of social media is a sign of our times and of people's expectations of others, including CEOs. It's not going to be acceptable anymore for the founder of a company to hide behind layers of bureaucracy, inaccessible and accountable to nobody. I get on Twitter and see if people are talking about the Butler Bag. When I first searched for people who are talking about me and responded to them in real time, I wondered, "Am I opening a can of worms? Can I keep up?" Then I realized that the most valuable thing I could do for my business is get to know these people. And you know what? They *love* when I contact them and thank them for the positive chatter. They think it's so cool that the CEO of the company has e-mailed or tweeted them. I truly appreciate them for supporting me, and that comes through.

In maintaining your brand, always question how you can best spend your time. To me, nothing is more important than creating authenticity and valuing your customers. You don't have to contact your customers every day to be authentic. Just following Butler Bag fans on Twitter and talking about what I'm doing on my mini-blog helps me to be authentic and transparent and to communicate.

Make the Personal Connection

Being a small company gives you a big advantage in being authentic, because you can connect with your customers on a personal level—something big corporations usually do not do well. For example, some people have told me that a big toy company will probably try to rip off Leader Girlz. But they can't, because they're not me. I'm a mother of little girls, a businesswoman, and an advocate for young girls' leadership. I can and do talk to my customers as a real person, not a corporate strategy. When a mom sees a doll that's a young girl in a leadership role put out by some megacorporation, it doesn't resonate with her. She assumes it's just more marketing from people who couldn't care less about young girls. But when a mom sees another mom who, out of her passion for her children, is trying to make a better world, it does resonate. You can't create or buy that, and it can be a huge advantage for you. Stay true to your passion and yourself, and don't shy away from the personal. Not being slick and corporate in this day and age is a big plus.

Authenticity is about putting yourself out there and taking chances. When I donate a bag to a charity, I never ask, "What am I getting back?" I take it on good faith that the organization is going to promote me in the best way possible. When you give to charity events, it shows that your company cares. But it's also about creating good karma. Put out generosity, and it will come back to you. They won't tell you that in business school, but it's the truth.

Know Your Core Values

Core values are the key to authentic branding. The core values of your company are what you model day after day. My employees see how I talk to customers on the phone, and they know that's how they need to act as well. My values—transparency, quality, authenticity, care for families, and inspiration—permeate every part of my company. As the leader of your company, your core values will do the same, so you'd better know what those values are and stick to them.

For example, last year I was cast for a reality show on Fox. I turned it down. The producers asked me to reconsider, and I told them I had said no because the show was against some of my core values. That spoke volumes to my employees and colleagues. It was an inspirational show, and it would have gotten my company great PR. But part of it didn't line up with my values. I would have had to be more showy about my lifestyle—display more expensive baubles and talk about how much money I spend—and expose parts of my private family life that I would rather keep private. It wouldn't have been me, so I said no. As Jim Collins writes in his latest best seller, *How the Mighty Fall: And Why Some Companies Never Give In*, violating core values in the undisciplined pursuit of more is one of the ways that companies fail.

Nothing will make your employees, colleagues, and customers dislike you more than being a hypocrite. If you do projects and support ways of doing business that violate everything you're supposed to stand for, then you're selling out your people and yourself. If you build your brand around being eco-friendly and 100 percent green but drive a Hummer as your personal vehicle, word will get out. In the age of the blog and social networking, your customers will rip you to shreds. Companies have been annihilated that way. Decide what's important to you, and make your business reflect those values no matter what the trends or the experts say.

Shaun Robinson from *Access Hollywood* wrote a book called *Exactly As I Am* about leadership and not giving in to media hype. It's a book that reflects her true values—values that are not always popular in her celebrity-driven business. After the book came out, when she appeared on *The Strategy Room* with me last year, the host of the show said, "Doesn't that make you a hypocrite when you hype up these celebrities? You are hyping up celebs on your show, and then in your book, you're telling these young girls not to believe the hype."

It's a tricky balancing act for Robinson, but what she's doing is really remarkable. She's pushing for change on her show. She now turns down segments like "Is Jessica Simpson getting fat?" or asks that they be restructured. She has become passionate about

WHAT IF? & WHY NOT?

empowering young girls. She's using her experience and passion to change how celebrity shows present news and information. Instead of being a hypocrite, she's turning it into a positive. She found that the only way she could go forward was to return to her core values and stand by them.

You Are Your Brand

One of the most rewarding things for me is when people meet me and say, "Wow, I feel like I know you. You're like one of my friends." That means I'm doing my job, which is to be the face of my brand. When you treat people with respect and consideration and give them your attention, they remember. They talk about how kind and thoughtful you were to them. That breeds brand loyalty.

Branding is everything you do. It's how you dress, how you speak, how you interact with others, what charities you give to, and what you drive. It's not a formula for getting your product into a swag suite with celebrities and getting your picture taken for *Us Weekly*. That's a microscopic part of it. When you start a company, you take on the responsibility of being a public person and living to a certain standard. Branding and marketing is an extension of you at all times.

You are your brand. If you try to sell your product first, I think you can have success, but the road will be much steeper and harder. Remember: people purchase based on emotion. If you can capture the emotion that led you to be inspired and start your company in the first place and then transmit that to others through your brand, you will inspire them to feel some of the same emotions about your idea that you feel. You will connect with them on an intimate, genuine level, and that vastly increases your chance of creating a lifelong customer.

Dreamer's Corner: A New Entrepreneur Q&A

Amy Sapirstein, Founder
activeurbanmom.wordpress.com
asapirstein@gmail.com

1. What is the name of your new business, and when did you start it?

Active Urban Mom LLC, which I started toward the end of 2007.

2. What type of business is it?

Active Urban Mom serves as the supporting brand for a product I created called Mommy Mitten. Mommy Mitten is a hand warmer that secures around the handlebar of baby strollers to keep moms' hands warm while pushing it out in cold/wet weather and even has a nifty zipper pocket to help moms keep track of keys, pacifiers, etc.

3. What was the greatest obstacle you faced in starting your business, and how did you overcome it?

My greatest obstacle has been time. I came up with this idea in October 2007 when my baby was just a couple of months old. Since I am a stay-at-home mom and do not have help during the day, I have been getting things accomplished while she naps or when she goes to bed at night. Trying to find time each day to get things accomplished while being mommy, wife, and homemaker is a challenge. Even so, I have worked through the patent process, trademarking, setting up an LLC, prototype creation, manufacturer selection, selecting a customs broker, getting a website built, and now implementing my marketing plan.

5. What is the most important lesson you have learned about starting a business?

I have learned that persistence and patience pay off. Maybe not monetarily (yet), but by helping me in gaining confidence, accomplishing things, and understanding my weaknesses, but more importantly, understanding my strengths.

(continued)

6. Where is your business today as far as earnings, size, etc.? What are your prospects for the future?

I am the only member of my company with no profits yet since selling has yet to begin. I have placed my initial bulk order, which should be complete and ready for sales by the end of summer 2009, just in time for the fall/winter season. My website is complete as well, but I did not launch it until summer to coincide with my product delivery.

A big part of my marketing plan includes leveraging social media and all it has to offer. I am working on introducing myself and my brand, Active Urban Mom, on Twitter, Facebook, and Cafémom and of course creating my own blog. My hope is to connect with urban moms and/or influencers to share my experiences, adventures, suggestions, and questions about living as an active new mom . . . and of course introducing Mommy Mitten when appropriate. I focus on the local New York City market, which I can approach in person via local mom groups, street fairs, word of mouth, and getting my product into some of the local boutiques. I love the in-person stuff!

What if viral marketing becomes all you need?

If there's one kind of marketing you should pursue, it's viral marketing. Viral marketing is when your message "infects" a community of people, and those people spread the message to everyone they know and even to people they don't know. You can imagine how powerful this is. Viral marketing is typically free, has the authenticity of coming from someone who doesn't have a financial stake in the company, and works for you 24/7. Almost any company or product can go viral, and if you find a way to get a viral buzz going for your business, take advantage.

Susan Boyle is a fantastic example of something going viral and becoming a huge overnight success. In case you don't recall, she was the homely looking Scottish lady who went on *Britain's Got*

Talent (the UK version of *American Idol*) in the spring of 2009 and shocked everyone with her gorgeous voice. People were so moved by her performance that within days millions had watched it on YouTube, and her story spread like the swine flu. Even though Ms. Boyle did not end up winning the show, no one was surprised when her first jazz CD came out.

Viral marketing usually starts with a story. Many know the story about the Butler Bag: I was a frustrated woman looking through my handbag for my keys. I finally grabbed the utensils basket out of the dishwasher and stuck it in my purse. That's a human story that people can understand. When I went on television and shared that story, and went on Facebook and Twitter, people heard the story and started sharing it with others: "Have you heard about the woman who invented this handbag by shoving her dishwasher tray in her purse?" The story had developed a life of its own.

I went to my grade school reunion a few years ago (yes, *grade* school reunion), and I had one of my bags with me. A girl came over and said, "Hey, is that a Butler Bag? I heard that the girl who created that company actually took the tray out of her dishwasher and stuck it into her bag!" One of my friends was with me and started giggling. I said, "Yes, that is exactly how my company got started." The woman was floored. But what blew me away was that she knew the story. She didn't know my name, but she knew my story, and that allowed her to share my story. That's still incredibly cool when it happens.

The best thing about viral marketing is that it's self-sustaining. Hotmail is the classic example. Once upon a time, it was an independent company, and the founders decided to give the mail service away. However, at the bottom of each e-mail was a signature line and hyperlink inviting the reader to create his or her own free Hotmail account. So Hotmail's users became salespeople for its service, leveraging their own e-mail address books. In 1998, Microsoft bought Hotmail for about $400 million, and today the service has more than 270 million users worldwide.

Here are some keys to creating a viral marketing buzz that can supercharge your company:

- *Give away products or services for free.* You want people talking about your company and brand, and to do that, they first have to experience what you have to offer.
- *Make it easy for people to tell others about you.* Have a great page on your website, for example, or a cool YouTube video that others can refer people to.
- *Target existing networks.* That's where Facebook and Twitter come in. If you can get your company talked about heavily on Facebook, you will see an uptick in business.
- *Engage the people who are talking about you.* When you see yourself praised via someone's Twitter feed, thank the person and offer him or her a gratitude gift. That will turn you into a hero.
- *Be real.* Viral marketing can work against you just as quickly as for you if you violate your core values. If the word on the street goes negative, you could find your business in big trouble.

Why not make social media the core of your viral marketing?

You may have figured out that I'm a big fan of Twitter and Facebook. If your core market is made up of people who live on the internet, then you may be able to center your branding on social networks like Facebook, MySpace, and Twitter. There are also others you can experiment with: LinkedIn, Bebo, hi5, Friendster, Reddit, Digg, and StumbleUpon, to name a few. There are hundreds of social networks, and there is nothing better for taking your brand viral.

I am always on Facebook and Twitter, networking and making relationships. For me, Twitter is a true business relationship. I have made many friends on Twitter, and they have become incredibly supportive of my business. They've helped me segment into new areas, bought products, booked me for radio and TV shows, signed me up for seminars, networked on my behalf, and helped me make new contacts. Social networking expedites the process of meeting people across the world. You multiply yourself dozens of times over just by being moderately active.

These are not passive tools. You can't just drop a profile on the sites and let it sit there, or nothing will happen. You have to engage. Share your story. Talk about your company. Tell people about what you're doing and where. Invite them to come see you speak. Get involved, create connections, and give advice. That's why it's called social "networking." If you're honest and genuine, people will like you and start talking about what you're doing. That's the first step to building a viral buzz online that can transform your company.

What if you turn out to be a natural marketer and speaker?

Many of the new entrepreneurs I speak with are nervous about the idea of being interviewed by a newspaper reporter or getting in front of a camera on a television show. Some are terrified. But it's amazing how many of them, when they get right down to it, are great spokespeople for their brands. You probably have a lot more poise and charisma than you think you do, and nobody is going to be a better spokesperson for your brand than you. That is why companies like QVC or HSN firmly believe that the best person to sell a product on-air is the creator (unless they have an incredible fear of being on television).

159

Once you get in front of an audience at a speaking engagement or do a TV segment on your local news channel, you find that people want you to succeed. They want to help you do your best, whether it's the kindly makeup artist at the TV station or the booker who sets you up to speak to a friendly crowd. Even your audience wants you to do well. When you realize that, it becomes easier to stop worrying about making a catastrophic mistake and just be yourself. Tell your story. Be who you are, focus on your intention, and connect with others. As I said earlier in the chapter, consumers are used to seeing professionals who appear "slick" on TV; what they really want is people who come across as real and normal—people with whom they can feel a connection.

Still, if you're uncertain about your poise in front of a camera or microphone, it's not a bad idea to get some coaching. Groups like Toastmasters (toastmasters.org) are wonderful for developing your speaking skills. As for the news media, you can hire a media coach to help you work on speaking slowly and clearly, refining your body language, polishing your talking points to be more concise and high-impact, and so on. If you can find someone with reasonable rates, that's money well spent if it helps you become a stellar company ambassador. Bottom line is, if you want to grow a brand you must push yourself to "get out there."

Why not create your own media coverage?

It's surprisingly easy to do if you're observant and opportunistic. Contact the editors or producers at all the media outlets where you would like to appear, and begin to build relationships with them. Write a segment or article pitch, and keep it concise. For example, let's say you're already big into Facebook and Twitter and would like to place a short article called "Five Ways Facebook Can Make You

More Organized" in *Real Simple* magazine to promote your home organization business. Here's how to go about it:

- E-mail the main editorial contact for *Real Simple*, and pitch your idea in a single sentence with a few bullet points to demonstrate your five brilliant tips. Include the length of the piece (shorter is better—maybe 200–300 words) and when you can deliver it. You can find submission guidelines for any magazine on its website.
- If the editor says she'd like to see it, write and send the article. Keep it the length you promised, include some online resources for the reader, and include your name, your company name, and your website address somewhere.
- Be patient. A response can take weeks.
- If the editor likes it, make whatever revisions are necessary, and send the final version.

The same standards apply for television as well.

Improve your odds by knowing what editors and producers want. Print publications typically need more short pieces than long: sidebars, callouts, factoids, and so on. For radio, you need to be able to provide some interesting interviews as part of your story. For television, your idea needs to be visual, so it's not just talking heads.

Sign up for Peter Shankman's HARO (Help a Reporter Out) list at helpareporter.com. Print editors, writers, and producers use this free service to put out regular bulletins to find what they are looking for in their next stories and broadcast segments. Getting on HARO's e-mail list will get you "in the know" so you can find regular high-profile opportunities for pitching your company and growing your brand. If you participate, make sure media professionals can contact you easily, and be ready to deliver when called.

These kinds of media placements can give your brand a major boost. *O, the Oprah Magazine* was doing a feature in January 2007 about the best organizing handbags. The editor of the magazine got online to research organized handbags. We had already been investing in Google AdWords for terms like "organized handbag." So when the editor Googled that phrase, there we were. The magazine called me in September of 2006, said they were doing the feature, and asked, "Could you send us a sample?" I think I broke the land speed record getting a bag to UPS. The magazine took the pictures, and in December of 2006, the article hit the stands with the Butler Bag featured. Good timing, being the holidays and all. It was a very exciting phone call when I heard that the magazine was out and my bag had made it. I will never forget where I was, what I was doing, and the time of day. We got a great sales boost for the month—but that was just the beginning.

The point is you can't stop at one placement. The buzz from Oprah fades. Once you create one press appearance, you must leverage that one to create more. We turned the Oprah story into retail buzz by sending retailers a copy of the article, but we also sent it to other editors. The news media is a collaborative community, and one editor's judgment affects the others. If an editor of one magazine deems you worth covering, then others will cover you, too. You may want to come up with a few different "hooks" for the different media outlets that appeal to different audiences. Follow these tips to maximize the value of your media coverage:

- Archive every media exposure you get—clippings, videotape, and audiotape—so that your website becomes a showcase of what you have been up to.
- Maintain a press area on your website where journalists can find press releases, streaming video and audio clips, a bio, company information, photos, and a schedule of your next appearances.
- If you want to send press releases, use free online press release distribution services like PRLog.org, free-press-release.com, 24-7pressrelease.com, PRbuzz.com, and PRleap.com.

- When you get high-profile coverage, immediately send copies, audio clips, or video clips to all the editors and producers in your press database. Let them know you're being covered. Also do the same for any retailers you are working with (or want to be working with) to continue the buzz.
- Remember that editors and producers need fresh, entertaining, original stories, and they need them fast. If every editor in your database rejects one idea, have five more ready to pitch. Read and watch what magazines, newspapers, radio programs, and TV shows are already running so you can come up with creative ideas that aren't already being used. When an editor or producer says yes to your pitch, be on the ball. Have your article written and ready to send. Be available to go to a studio and be interviewed the *same day*. Have high-quality digital photos of your products on hand to e-mail to a reporter.

If you want to invest a little money and get amazing PR leads, subscribe to ProfNet at profnet.prnewswire.com. It's a subscription service that allows you to get requests for expert commentary from more than 14,000 journalists and other communications professionals seeking expert sources. Opportunities to be part of articles and broadcast features for major media outlets just appear in your e-mail inbox. It's a fabulous way to be part of major press coverage before your competitors even know it exists. HARO is free, but if you have the cash to spare, join both lists, and you'll get even more fabulous press leads. Once again, being prepared and quick to respond is crucial.

In addition, try the "local celebrity" strategy. Focus your attention on the news media just in your home metropolitan area. Contact them when you're ready to launch your company, and see if they want to do a story in the "local boy/girl makes good" vein. Newspapers and local radio stations especially are eager to do features on local people. That could be the coverage that starts the ball rolling for you.

What if there are ways to publicize your business for next to nothing?

Viral marketing is free other than the cost of giving away some product. Being on Facebook and Twitter is free other than the time you spend. If you are your own publicist at first, then any media coverage you generate is free. Just being out there every day talking with customers is your best advertising, because you are a walking billboard for your business at all moments. Public speaking is a also a very effective way of building your brand and connecting with people. I've said that you need to know everything you can about branding; the same is true for PR. *Where's My Fifteen Minutes?* by Howard Bragman is a must-read for gaining insight into the world of public relations, how it works, and how to generate coverage.

I have never spent a dime on traditional broadcast or print advertising. I don't feel it has emotional appeal or a personal touch, it's difficult to track its effectiveness, and it's expensive. Instead, my company donates to events such as charity auctions. We get our products into the hands of people who will talk about them. I've had my Butler Bags in major celebrity swag suites, where celebs come before big events like the Oscars to pick up items that companies want them to talk about. In those cases, the only real costs are the bags themselves and the cost of traveling to the event to hand out my product personally.

I was at a Hollywood event with dozens of other companies that make fashion and beauty items—bags, cosmetics, jewelry, and so on. But on the first day that the suite was open, I was the only woman there wearing a classy black dress and power pumps with my hair done and makeup done—the only one who was "TV ready." Almost every other woman was in jeans and casual shoes. To dress up was a decision I made consciously, because I knew that I could be photographed and that news outlets would be walking through on the hunt for celebrities. I wanted to look like I was ready for the spotlight. That day, I got several TV interviews and I had my picture taken with lots of celebrities who remembered my bags and talked about them. You can guess what happened the next day: every other woman who had products in that suite was dressed to the nines.

My fashion strategy didn't cost much. But it paid off big time in celebrity buzz, pictures for my website, and new connections. People got to know me and my brand because of low-cost tricks like that.

Why not use "seed marketing"?

Getting product into swag suites is just one aspect of a strategy known as "seed marketing," or experience marketing. Seed marketing basically means that you take your brand and product into an environment and bring people into contact with it. You create an experience for them that makes them love what you're selling. Then they seek you out and tell other people about you. You should be sprinkling seeds all the time everywhere and constantly watering. Some won't grow, which is why you plant a bunch. This is about not being the lone entrepreneur in the back room; it's about getting out there, meeting people, touting your brand, and connecting with your market.

Red Bull does seed marketing brilliantly. The company builds its brand on being a sponsor and partner at events and by creating a live experience for the consumer. Red Bull sponsors wild events like cliff diving and human-powered flying machine competitions, and provides its energy drinks to the spectators. So you're downing Red Bull while you're present at something totally unique, and you connect that feeling of coolness and adventure with the brand. Advertising just shouts at the consumer and is easily forgotten; seed marketing creates personal experiences that people remember.

During the writing of this book, I was at the opening night of the Gen Art Film Festival with about a thousand people.

Neutrogena was one of the sponsors. At the party afterward, Neutrogena was doing makeup for the women. Genius! Many of them were wearing makeup when they came to the event, but they sat through a movie in the dark and now were walking into a bar and wanted to have a fresh look. So Neutrogena gave them the experience and then a goody bag of things to take home. Three Olives was also there, and its Cherry-tini drinks were everywhere you looked. On the bar the company had a lighted logo that really stood out.

I don't know how much it cost Neutrogena or Three Olives to be there, but that's how you get customers. They created an emotional experience and didn't ask anyone to buy anything. As a result, people loved them. People loved Neutrogena's makeup and probably bought a bunch of its products that week. Make-Up Art Cosmetics (MAC) uses the same strategy in that it offers free makeovers all the time. I go there to get makeup done, and whenever I go, I always buy something—lipstick, lip liner, eyeliner—always something. The Apple Store uses the idea as well. Each store has a Genius Bar where experts show you things for free. I've been blown away by the cool factor of that experience: "You mean I could do that with my MacBook, too?" It's about experiences.

Could you use your product or service to create experiences that would generate affinity? I'll bet you could. Be creative; you don't need to have a cosmetics or liquor company to do it. If you sell pet-grooming products and services, try holding a public grooming day for elderly or ill people who can't hold a squirming, wet dog. If you run a bakery, donate muffins or other goods to a big community event and stick a little stake with your name and phone number in each muffin. There are many ways to create delight and joy that people will remember you for. Remember, you do not just want to create the experience for that moment but also provide a way to extend and continue the relationship that you've put so much effort into beginning.

Lessons Learned

► Branding is the most important part of launching your company.

► You are your brand.

► Branding is everything you do that connects emotionally with your customers and their needs. Marketing is the activity that communicates your brand's message.

► The four keys to success are knowing your market, understanding their needs and wants, finding creative ways to connect with them, and being consistent.

► You should connect with your market through multiple branding channels.

► You are your best marketer.

► Authenticity is the most important aspect of any brand.

► Social networking sites are incredible tools for connecting with others and going viral.

► You are your own best publicist. Even if you hire a PR team, you need to know PR inside and out.

► There are many ways of marketing and creating press coverage for little or no money.

► Seed marketing, which is creating experiences for others, has made companies like Red Bull into powerhouses.

The Next Twenty-Four

In the next twenty-four hours . . .

✓ Research old ideas that bombed but could be resurrected.

✓ Write out your core values.

✓ Write down the branding and marketing channels you already have in place—website, e-mail list, networking, speaking engagements, and so on.

✓ Create your company's Facebook and Twitter profiles.
✓ Research media contacts whose e-mail request lists you want to join.
✓ Create a list of your hometown media to contact about press coverage of your business.
✓ List possible ways you could do seed marketing.

My Dream Plan, Part 7

Write down your brand development strategy.

A sentence that describes my brand:

_____

_____

_____

_____

The five words that capture my brand's appeal:

_____

_____

_____

_____

The five channels that would be best for building my brand:

_____

_____

_____

_____

My strategy for going viral:

_____

_____

_____

_____

My strategy for generating press coverage:

_____

_____

_____

_____

"What if I'm terrified of selling and don't think I'm good at it?"

8

Without people to go out and sell its products and services, every business would dry up and blow away. You can have incredible branding and marketing and a brilliant business strategy, but if you're going to make it, you need someone on the streets shaking hands, making deals, and bringing in money. When your business is just starting, that someone is probably going to be you. And that's where many entrepreneurs get really nervous. They think selling is about pressure, sleazy tactics, arm-twisting, and scenes right out of *Glengarry Glen Ross*. But that's not what sales is about at all. In this chapter, I share with you the reality of sales, and once you've seen it in a more accurate light, you'll no longer be nervous about it.

Overcoming Sales Phobia

Many entrepreneurs dread sales more than any other aspect of doing business. But that's because they have a misunderstanding of what sales is. People will tell you that selling is about creating demand where it doesn't exist, but that's not what selling really is. This is my definition of selling:

Solving problems and creating opportunities.

Doesn't that give sales an almost noble quality? Even the most silver-tongued sales professional can't make someone buy based only on pressure and "get the signature" tactics. But if he or she can position the product or service in a way that makes the customer's business or life easier, better, or more rewarding, the sales will flood in. So think about your business from that perspective: "What problems do I solve for people, and what opportunities do I bring?"

Once you start thinking in this way, it will become much easier to get out and sell. Because instead of feeling like you are trying to part people from their hard-earned income, you will feel buoyed by the fact that you're trying to improve business or life for somebody else. You're trying to help someone solve a problem, and you may even inspire him or her along the way.

For example, let's say that you have your massage therapist's license, and your vision is to open a mobile therapeutic massage studio that would travel to companies and provide on-site massages. Before you make your first calls to schedule appointments, think about the problem you're offering to solve for the companies that hire you: stressed-out employees. That will completely change your pitch to human resources directors. You might even produce a mailer or website outlining how massage can save a company money by reducing absenteeism and improving productivity. Instead of going into the sales process thinking, "How can I get you to give me your money?" you'll think, "Here's everything I can do for you." Always acknowledge what "the problem" is and how or why you can solve that problem. If you're offering real value, the deal should almost close itself.

Fear of selling is normal, but you have to get past it if you are the owner of the company. One great way to get past it is to reframe it in your mind: you're not hawking a product; you're building a brand. You're not selling a service; you're selling a vision. You're coming to people with passion about an opportunity.

I personally don't like selling, but the way I got over that was to remind myself that I was giving buyers a chance to benefit from my idea and company. When I went out to sell the Butler Bag, my focus was on the problem my idea could solve for retailers: how to appeal to busy women who desperately want a way to stay organized while remaining fashionable. For the most part, handbags were one or the other: stylish or utilitarian. There wasn't really a product that blended the two, so I created one and sold it as something that would give retailers and licensees an entrée to a new segment of the market. It worked. Suddenly, I wasn't just selling a handbag; I was selling a lifestyle that retailers knew would resonate with their buyers. More importantly, I realized being a storyteller is more effective than being a salesperson.

It Has to Be You

In the beginning, if you're nervous about selling, you might be tempted either to find a partner who can handle sales for you or contract your sales to an outside sales company (more on that later). Don't. Initially, you should be doing your own selling, even if it scares the daylights out of you. There are several good reasons to consider this:

- *You need to control costs and raise cash.* When you're launching, you don't have the budget to hire someone, and you can't afford to give away 20 percent to a sales agency or sales team.
- *It's the best way to learn about business.* Handling your own sales does more than save you money; it teaches you about business. When you spend the first six months getting your own leads and closing your own deals, you're going to learn

more than you would in three years of business school: contracts, distribution, fulfillment, packaging, quality control, and beyond. You'll also learn how to deal with all kinds of people and sales objections and how to circumvent them, and how to make your company better.

- *Nobody knows your product or company better than you.* When you're doing your own sales, you don't have to bring anybody up to speed on your products, future plans, or value propositions. You already know them.

- *Nobody is as passionate about your product or company.* This is one of the most important factors. You can feel it in the people I've profiled in the Dreamer's Corner features. These people love their businesses and the freedom and opportunity their ideas have created. That makes them their own best salespeople. When you love your business, other people feel that and respond to it.

- *You need to overcome your fear.* Before you get out there and start selling, you're like an actor who's nervous backstage, but like that actor, when you are finally in front of the audience and doing what you do best, the fear vanishes. When you're connecting with a customer about your wonderful idea and all the ways it can benefit him or her, you'll be amazed at how easy selling can be. It will also give you the opportunity to continue to increase your self-esteem and confidence.

Start Slowly

When someone launches a company that is product-driven, he or she says, "I want my product on QVC or in Target." But it's important to crawl before you walk. Yes, your goal might be to get on QVC or into large retailers like Target, but you don't try to do that first. You probably won't know how to handle that kind of deal yet. There is a great deal to learn, from delivering merchandising support materials to managing quality assurance. When you're playing in the big leagues, you can get in big-league trouble if you make mistakes. For example, if you deliver a product of subpar quality to QVC, they may fine you, and they might ship all your units back, sticking you with the cost. Plus, they may never want to do business with you again.

If you're selling products, the first thing you should do is sell online. The bar is set low, and it's a great venue in which to learn, without as many expectations. This allows you to work out the bugs in your business model and develop some momentum without risking any disasters. You'll find out how much it costs to ship something and how to ship products safely and cost-effectively. You'll discover the best way to handle customer relations and returns. And you'll start generating cash flow, which is critical.

After that, start creating relationships with other small businesses that can sell your products. Stick with small, boutique companies at first, because they are run by entrepreneurs like you, so they don't have the stringent rules or bureaucracy of big corporations. When you're working with a mom-and-pop company, you can make mistakes and the owners will forgive you because they probably made the same mistakes when they were starting out. Often, these small companies will actually help you learn through the process. They become partners in your mutual success, and that is the best kind of seller/buyer relationship to have.

Even if you are in a service business and you're not shipping product, you should always test-drive your business model by starting with small sales. In a service business like graphic design or personal shopping, you are the product. But you still have many questions to answer. How do you bill for your time? What is your deliverable? What are your hours? How many clients can you and should you take on at once? Starting with smaller clients is like giving a new boat a shakedown cruise—it gives you a chance to find and fix the leaks before you go after the big-dollar, high-stakes clients who are a lot less forgiving.

The Sale Is Just the Beginning

It's one thing to get an account but another thing to keep it. Making a sale is not the end of your work; it's the beginning. Selling creates a relationship, but the customer is looking to you to maintain that relationship. Once the contract is signed, the pressure is on you to move from selling to *servicing*—solving the problems you claimed you could solve. If you can't, there are many other businesses that would be happy to take your place. That's another reason it is so valuable to handle your own sales when your business is starting out. Early customers are your most important customers, since they will enable you to survive. You need to get to know them and learn how you can best meet their needs because they help you to create the processes that become part of your business operations. It's important to regard sales as the first level of a multitiered, long-term partnership between you and your customer.

Tier One is when you are simply a supplier and the customer is buying your products. The relationship might not go any deeper than that, but that doesn't mean you don't have a lot of responsibilities. If you're in a business like mine, in which you sell a product to others who will resell it, then you must do whatever it takes to create maximum "sell-through." That's the pace at which your products move off the shelves and turn into revenue for your customer. High sell-through means happy customers; if you don't create sell-through, you won't get that account again, and the customer may lose trust in your brand.

My company takes it as our job to create sell-through for the retailer. That's why we do things like sending a media stand and constantly refreshing it with new articles and information about features of the Butler Bag. If you're dealing with the retail channel, then you must become a master merchandiser. Go to the stores, talk to managers, talk to the customers, and get in the trenches. Find out what helps attract a consumer to a product and what helps close the sale. That might mean creating point-of-purchase (POP) materials, signage, hang tags, and other things to help move product. Plan on supplying marketing and POP tools; if you don't, you are losing sales. We give what we call "demo" handbags to every one of our stores so they can display the Butler Bag organizational system. A lot of people think that's a big expense, but that bag is a small cost in comparison to all the sales it can drive, because it allows us to partner with those stores more effectively. In merchandising, you spend a few dollars to make a lot more dollars.

If the product sells best when demonstrated, plan on training and paying people to go to stores and demo it. If video works well, then plan on shooting a high-quality video demo and sending DVDs to every retailer. It's an investment in making your product something that creates strong revenue for your customers. When you can do that, you'll make more sales. Additionally, you want to be working on your PR and social media campaigns daily. The more you get out there and build your brand, the more it will drive traffic to your stores and partners and produce more sell-through.

Tier Two is customer service. If you're starting a service business, you'll go directly to this stage, because you are your product. Customer service is incredibly important, because when you make a sale, you are promising, "I will be there for you when you need me." That means you'd better be there. How many times have you liked a company until you needed its help and were stuck on the phone for an hour only to receive no assistance? How did you feel about the company after that? If you're in a service business, Tier Two begins the moment the client says, "You're hired." Then you must meet the obligations set down by your brand. Typically, that means the following.

- Meeting your deadlines
- Being punctual
- Doing what you say you will do
- Maintaining open communication

- Handling changes or revisions quickly and gladly; being flexible
- Billing fairly and accurately
- Delivering extra value

Delivering extra value means exceeding expectations, or, as some call it, "under-promising and over-delivering." If you say that a job will be done in six hours, finish it in five. If you fix someone's laptop computer, return it with some virus protection software added free of charge. Those are the types of small gestures that create long-term customer loyalty and generate referrals.

If you're in a product-based business, more often than not customer service will involve solving problems and handling complaints: the item is too small, the packaging doesn't fit on the shelves, the quality is substandard, customers can't figure out how to work it, the shipment didn't arrive on time, and so on. Whenever you are faced with a customer-service challenge like these, your policy should be simple:

Do whatever it takes to make it right.

Customers will judge your company not on what it does when things are going well, but on what you do when things go wrong. Companies that point fingers, deny, blame, or just give customers the runaround have trouble staying in business very long. On the other hand, I have seen many small businesses that screwed up big time and then went to such extraordinary lengths to fix the problem that their customers came to appreciate them more than they ever would have if there hadn't been a disaster. So when a customer-service crisis hits, remember the Five A's:

1. Accept responsibility for what happened, possibly even if you don't think you're at fault.

2. Apologize. "I'm so sorry that this happened. I can understand why you're upset, and we are going to make this right as quickly as possible."
3. Address the problem quickly by whatever means necessary—paying for repairs, redoing work, and so on.
4. Appreciate the customer's having let you know that you were falling short and helping you become a better company. Send a formal thank you like a card or gift basket.
5. Analyze what happened and why. Take steps to make sure it doesn't happen again.

Tier Three comes when you and your customer have been through the wars together and built a level of mutual trust. This is when you will begin to become more like partners than buyer and seller. You'll begin creating new products or services together, perhaps engaging in joint ventures or launching new companies. This is a wonderful place to arrive at, and it will come about in its own time.

Dreamer's Corner: A New Entrepreneur Q&A

Nancy Guberti, Founder
www.coachforhealthyliving.com
nancy@coachforhealthyliving.com

1. What is the name of your new business, and when did you start it?

Coach for Healthy Living officially launched in 2004.

2. What type of business is it?

We are experts in wellness programs for corporations, academic institutions, and individuals. Our Twelve-Step program empowers people to lead

(continued)

healthy lifestyles, and our specialized workshops address conditions such as autism, celiac disease, cancer, and weight loss. We also will be offering a private line of health-related products such as organic baby formula for newborns and infants, high-protein superfood breakfast drinks for active adults, and instant breakfast drinks for seniors.

3. What was the greatest obstacle you faced in starting your business, and how did you overcome it?

Time management: determining the most important tasks to be done and creating an organizational chart to keep me on track with what tasks need to get accomplished when and how. Setting goals and reviewing them weekly is often helpful.

4. What has the experience of being an entrepreneur taught you about yourself, and how has it changed you?

After spending over fifteen years on Wall Street at major brokerage firms including Morgan Stanley, Credit Suisse First Boston, Lehman Brothers, and Goldman Sachs, I found myself driven in another career direction. When my youngest son was diagnosed with a liver disorder and numerous allergies, I felt compelled to intervene when doctors did not offer much hope. I closed the chapter of my career life at Goldman and went to study for my master's in nutrition while researching with scientists worldwide to find a cure for my son's condition. My work ethic helped me endure long days and nights and stay focused. The final result was nothing short of a miracle, and it changed me as well, so CoachforHealthyLiving.com was born. I offer private consultations as well as corporate wellness programs. Now this is more mission than career, empowering others to lead a healthier lifestyle utilizing noninvasive tests, educational seminars, and tried-and-true products. Switching careers at any age has its challenges, but persistence and love of the mission is imperative.

5. What is the most important lesson you have learned about starting a business?

You have to wear all the hats at the beginning. At Goldman Sachs, if I was having computer issues, I'd call the tech department. If I needed to travel,

I'd call the travel department. I received a paycheck no matter what. With running your own business, you have to do everything until you can hire employees. Performance reviews occur every day.

6. **Where is your business today as far as earnings, size, etc.?**
Besides more clients and corporate wellness accounts, we are launching a product line. In addition, I have a GFCF cookbook for autism spectrum disorders, an audio CD outlining twelve steps to a healthier lifestyle and a 365-day health living calendar. I've been a keynote speaker at a national autism seminar and the Holistic Moms Network.

What if your product or service virtually sells itself?

In 2005, the company Beachbody and trainer Tony Horton came out with a home fitness program called P90X. This is nothing unusual; there are a million home fitness products out there being sold via infomercial. But something about this product made it special. For one thing, it worked. The company has kept running infomercials for P90X to this day, but its best sales tool has been its users. They are evangelists for the program; it's not unusual to hear people talking about P90X on airplanes, in Facebook status updates, in dozens of online fitness forums, and in restaurants wherever you go. It's remarkable. That's an example of a product selling itself. It's one of the reasons that P90X has become the best-selling fitness program of all time.

Your product or service may have that kind of potential. You can't know until you get out there and let others become familiar with it. If it does sell itself, then all you need to do is make sure it gets in front of the right people—the influencers and the ones with the ability to write a check. How do you know if your product has that power? It's a hard thing to quantify or predict, but here are some persuasive things to look for that might suggest you could have a self-selling hit on your hands:

- Your product or service offers obvious value.
- It's unlike anything else on the market and solves a problem.
- People get very excited about it and tell others (it goes viral).
- It's linked to something important happening in the wider culture (such as a topical book or a President Obama poster during the 2008 election).

But, again, you won't really know if your product sells itself until you get out there, make some sales, and find out what people are saying. That's another great reason to make social networking sites part of your strategy. They give you the power to follow what others are saying about you and to have a better idea of whether or not your product or service is becoming self-sustaining. You can also use Technorati (technorati.com) to follow what's being said about you in blogs. So get out there and make a few sales, and see what happens! Make sure you always use the feedback you receive as a tool to keep improving.

Why not cultivate a solid-gold referral base that makes selling even more automatic?

Referrals are, hands down, the best way to market your business, build your brand, and make new sales. The referral can come from a friend or colleague or even a feature in a magazine. That's because, unlike advertising, referrals come from real people who have no vested interest in making you more sales. They just tell other people about your product or service because they like it and are excited about it. But you can use referrals to get you in the door more easily and to have customers presold on you before you walk in the door.

You should be working to create a base of credible people who will talk you up within the industry in which you are trying to sell. For example, if you're looking to make sales within the apparel industry, then you should be attending apparel trade shows (more likely as a guest than a vendor) and networking events, handing out samples of your products, speaking at round tables, writing articles, and doing everything possible to get your name known in the industry. Spend time talking with key figures in the sector, and impress them with your knowledge and passion. Make sure you're a member of LinkedIn and other business networking websites.

Eventually, some of those people are going to start talking about you to others in their organizations. You will become known as a sharp operator who makes great products, has valuable insights, and/or is just a lot of fun to be around. It doesn't really matter what they say about you as long as it's positive. What you want to do is reduce the sales resistance of the person who's going to be saying yes or no when you call to get an appointment. If that someone hears that you're sharp and easy to talk to and really know the business, he or she will probably be eager to meet you.

Even better is to have a base of customers who adore you, your product, your service, and your brand. Create a forum on your website for customers to post comments. Tell new contacts they can learn more about you on your site, and let them find the glowing comments on their own. Get testimonials from your happiest clients, and print them on the back of your business cards. Offer old customers rewards for referring you new customers. Once you have a cadre of raving fans, they will become your de facto sales force.

Of course, keep in mind that the opposite is also true: if you mistreat a customer, you will dump poison into your market and damage your business. In fact, one angry customer has more power than ten thrilled customers, because people are more likely to tell others about their negative experiences. That's a great reason to make sure your customer service is always stellar.

What if You're a Natural Salesperson?

In the beginning, you may have no choice but to be your company's sole salesperson. But I have seen this scenario again and again: a new entrepreneur, scared to death of dipping his or her toe into the cold waters of selling, does it because there's nobody else, loves it, and takes to the water like Michael Phelps. That could be you. There are plenty of entrepreneurs out there who have what it takes to be natural sales stars.

Selling doesn't take a loud voice, an aggressive personality, or any of the other clichéd qualities you've seen in the movies. Are you a natural salesperson? If you have three or more of the following qualities, I'd say you are.

- You like spending time with people.
- You're a great listener.
- You think well on your feet.
- You're good at solving problems and improvising.
- You're persistent.
- You're deeply passionate about your business and your vision.

If you don't have three or more of these qualities, then you may not be the best person to sell your business—at least, not today. In that case, you could get low-cost sales training through an organization like Sales Practice (salespractice.com), learn by reading classic sales books like *The Little Red Book of Selling* by Jeffrey Gitomer, or if you're convinced you're simply not suited to sell, hire a sales rep or outsource your sales to a contractor (but this should be a last resort).

There is one book I believe every person should read, and especially entrepreneurs embarking on their journey: *How to Win*

Friends and Influence People by Dale Carnegie. This book is a classic, and I do not know many successful entrepreneurs who have not read it. It teaches you the art of successful people skills, and after all, that's what sales is all about: relating to people, finding their needs by being a good listener, and offering to help them find solutions.

Nobody will ever sell your company like you will. Remember what I said previously—true selling isn't about pressure. It is about relating to others, building trust, and convincing them that you're on their side and that your success equals their success. The best salespeople find creative ways to talk to the decision maker for a business and have a knack for getting others just as excited about their vision as they are. How will you know if you're a born salesperson? There's only one way: get out there and try it! You might like it.

What if People Will Actually Welcome You When You Call?

One reason that so many new entrepreneurs fear selling is because they assume that everyone in the business world is hostile to selling. That might be true in a few cases, but when you really look at the idea, it doesn't make sense. Sales are the lifeline for many companies. How would a company that uses a high volume of photocopies function if it didn't have a Ricoh salesman coming along every two weeks to take a new order and hear about the latest technical issues? What would an advertising agency do without a regular flow of freelance designers coming along trying to get work on ad campaigns?

Sales calls aren't unwelcome. *Salespeople* sometimes are. If you are pushy or deceptive or don't listen, you won't be welcome at someone's place of business, but then again, you also wouldn't be welcome on a first date. One of the best ways to overcome sales phobia is to demystify the process. It's not magic. It's creating a relationship. If you bring something worthwhile to the relationship, people will welcome you and be more willing to give you their business.

Here are some of the best ways to get your foot in the door and have purchasing directors, retailers, and other customers happy to see you:

- *Leverage people you know.* Make your initial contact via a mutual friend, or a customer or employee of the company who already knows you. Having someone else introduce you acts as a kind of testimonial. Your credibility soars.
- *Offer advance notice.* Let the person to whom you'll be talking know ahead of time that you'll be calling on him or her to try to make a sale. Be direct about it: "I'd love to meet with you in a month to talk about signing a contract with your company."
- *Send samples or information well in advance.* Nobody likes to be caught flat-footed. Give the person with whom you'll be meeting time to figure you out.
- *Be polite, punctual, positive, and considerate.* Bring good energy to the room. Ask about the other person's day, family, and background. Find cues in the conversation that you can use to create common ground, such as learning that you went to college in the same town.
- *Provide a start and end time for your meeting.* Promise to be in and out in twenty minutes because you respect the person's time. If he or she likes what you're saying, he or she will ask you to stay longer.
- *Don't pressure.* State your case, make your value proposition clear, ask for the sale, and then say farewell. If you've got something they want, they'll contact you. Not applying pressure suggests confidence.
- *Follow up.* E-mail or write to thank the person for his or her time.

You may run into some decision makers who naturally like people and enjoy the give and take of sales. That's great. But more often than not, you'll need to *make* yourself the kind of salesperson who's welcomed and whose visits are anticipated, even by the busy decision makers who will be signing the contracts. It's hard work, but if you can manage it, you'll find selling easier and more rewarding.

Why Not Ultimately Outsource Your Sales?

If you have a product or service with benefits that are obvious and customers who are passionate, *eventually* you might be better off contracting with a sales agency and spending your time on PR, development, and networking.

New entrepreneurs often struggle with whether or not to hire an outside sales group to sell their products. Some don't even know this option exists, but it does. Companies like OnCall LLC, MarketStar, and Acquirent make their living handling sales for other companies as independent contractors. As I've said, in the beginning, it makes sense for you to handle your own sales because it's the best business classroom you will ever find. You need to hear why people are and aren't buying your product. Also, you don't need sales reps all over the country, because with the internet, you can e-mail prospects information in seconds. But at some point, it may make sense to outsource your sales. When?

First of all, you're not ready for an outside sales team until you have your quality-control system operating smoothly. You cannot afford any quality issue when someone else is representing you. Second, you're ready for a sales team when you are ready to expand. When you want to add an office or launch new products but don't have the cash coming in to increase your expenditures, boosting sales is a great alternative for raising capital, and an outside sales force can often increase sales by sending more reps into the field. But before you bring in outside reps, make sure you have a lot of product to give them. They will need to give away a lot of freebies to create demand and interest.

If you are ready, hiring an external sales force can be a huge asset. Expect to pay from a 15 percent to 25 percent commission. Most companies typically work on commission only, though some may ask for a fee up front, like a retainer. I personally do not work with these companies. I favor the 100 percent commission model because the contractor has a financial stake in the results. If they don't produce, you're not on the hook for anything. If they do produce, everybody wins.

Having a team of professional sales reps out there working for you full time can be a huge asset. Just be sure that you choose an agency that "gets it" and understands your brand, your passion, and you.

Why Not Build a Brand That Does 90 Percent of the Selling for You?

If you build a brand that is unique, emotionally appealing, clear, and consistent, it will break a fresh trail for you toward the big sales that will make your company expand. It will also make it easier for you to be your own salesperson. Brands that are "built to sell" are the ones that are impossible to escape, because they're constantly being talked about. They are in the news media, in the online buzz, and in conversation at professional events and power lunches. When people hear the name of the brand, they know immediately what it is and what it stands for. When you can create a brand with that kind of visibility and ubiquity, you'll go into any sales meeting 90 percent presold.

Sara Blakely and Spanx are a great example of this. Sara created a product line that filled a need for women, but beyond that, Sara went out and told her story about why and how she created the brand. The media loved the story and the fact that the brand embodied women solving problems. In turn, the products sold themselves, and Spanx has become a trusted brand known for help-ing women look their best.

There is no reason your brand can't do the same thing. Your brand does the selling when it creates an impression in the minds of buyers that your product or service provides something that they simply cannot do without. "Brand equals demand" is another way of putting it. Your brand is close to that level when it is associated with unfailing quality and exceptional value for the money and when it says something desirable about its target customer.

What brands fall into that category today? How about Dom Perignon, Nike, Tiffany, and Four Seasons, for starters? Nobody has to sell those brands. Their customers show up presold by the brand equity and the feeling inherent in owning a product carrying the brand's story and characteristics. You may not be able to be Levi's overnight, but your brand can have the same kind of impact on a smaller scale and grease the sales wheels in the same way.

Lessons Learned

- ▶ Most people are scared of selling at first; it's normal.
- ▶ You are your own best salesperson.
- ▶ Remember to approach sales as a storyteller.
- ▶ Selling is about creating opportunities, solving problems, and inspiring people.
- ▶ Starting slow teaches you about all that's involved in deliver-ing a product to a buyer.
- ▶ The sale is just the beginning of the relationship.
- ▶ It's your job to provide your customers with the market-ing and sell-through tools they need.
- ▶ Some people welcome sales calls.
- ▶ Referrals can be your best sales force.
- ▶ A great brand presells you to your buyer.

The Next Twenty-Four

In the next twenty-four hours . . .

✓ List the reasons you're afraid of selling.
✓ List the reasons you might be great at it.
✓ Begin reading at least one classic sales book, such as *Never Eat Alone* by Keith Ferrazzi, *Close Like the Pros* by Steve Marx, *Take the Cold Out of Cold Calling* by Sam Richter, and *How to Master the Art of Selling* by Tom Hopkins.
✓ Brainstorm ways you could create a referral base.
✓ Research at least three contract sales companies.

My Dream Plan, Part 8

Outline your sales strategy.

Who will handle my sales:

_____

_____

_____

_____

My ideal customers will be:

_____

_____

_____

_____

I will get leads from:

_____

_____

_____

_____

I will create the following sales materials:

_____

_____

_____

_____

I will support my customers by offering:

_____

_____

_____

_____

I will create a strong referral base by:

_____

_____

_____

_____

"What if the business isn't immediately profitable?"

9

I am very right-brained, so the money side of business is not that much fun for me. It became fun when someone explained to me that managing cash flow, budgeting, and dealing with red ink—all the things I didn't like to do—made brainstorming, innovating, and brand development—all the things I love doing—possible.

Numbers are the key to your company, because the more revenue you have, the more freedom you have to experiment and invent and revolutionize your industry. The more you risk and the more you spend to create a winning brand, the higher your potential to do great things. Still, it's important to acknowledge that it's very possible your business won't be profitable right away. That's perfectly okay. You'll make it through the money-losing period just like thousands of other entrepreneurs have done.

Deficits Equal Motivation

Business finance is usually not fun in the beginning, because all you're likely to see is red ink. However, understanding those numbers helps you come up with better strategies and plans for execution. Knowing that you have money going out and need to create money coming in keeps you from becoming complacent. It pushes you to be creative and bring in more revenue from more sources: new products, services, consulting, and the like. The pressure of the numbers forces you to act, be bold, and take risks, and those are good things. But you have to accept that when you're starting out, especially if you're bootstrapping your new venture, things are going to be tight.

You can get through the rough launch period, but it will be easier if you understand your cash flow and receivables and how to manage them. Do not accept "net 30" payments on new accounts (meaning they pay you thirty days after you provide the service or product), because as a new company you need the instant cash flow. On the flip side, try to get net 30, 60, or 90 payment agreements for your accounts with vendors that are providing you a service. This will allow you to build more cash flow before you have to pay your bills. More established companies can often extend this opportunity if they want to build a long-term relationship with you.

I also suggest that you reduce your personnel costs by compensating new hires by giving them an ownership share in the company that vests over time and/or profit sharing, rather than a salary. This allows you to add new partners with important skill sets for no money up front. If this isn't acceptable to the people you want, try giving them a reduced salary with equity or performance bonuses. As I mentioned previously, if people have "skin in the game," they will be more motivated to help the company grow and prosper.

Here's an example: The girl in my company who makes sure every order goes out—she hand-checks the quality and makes sure that all the customer thank-you cards are in the boxes—gets a small portion of the value of every box that goes out as a bonus. So by the end of the day, she makes sure that all the boxes that can go out at our standard of quality *do* go out. If something is returned for improper packing or contents, she could lose money. Do you think she's motivated? She's not just clocking in; she's a part of the company's growth. She's excited every time a new sale comes in. Giving your employees a role in creating more cash flow can really help boost productivity and morale.

Give Your Business Enough Oxygen

Overestimate the amount of capital you will need at the start. A lot of companies fail because they are underfunded. If you decide to get funding from an outside source like family or an SBA loan, make sure you get at least 20 percent more than your business plan calls for. You are infusing your company with cash like a heart-lung machine infuses a body with blood and oxygen. Without enough cash to handle down periods and inevitable crises, your company can die.

However, the extra cash doesn't necessarily have to come from a source outside your company. If it does, you may be just giving your company away to an investor, and we've already talked about the dangers of that. How else can you infuse your company with cash? You do it by working your cash flow. Once you have created cash flow, then learn to manage invoicing so that you are being paid in thirty days or less while paying your suppliers and service providers over a longer period. That gives you some breathing space to use the incoming cash to manufacture, pack, and ship new orders for your vendors before you have to pay.

Licensing, co-marketing, and partnering are also ways of infusing capital into your business, but people just don't think of them that way. Infusion is:

any activity that brings a significant new flow of revenue into your company without substantively increasing your costs.

For example, if you are launching a new product and you have a friend whose organization has a similar market, propose a joint venture. This is co-marketing as infusion. The people who buy my bags want to be organized. I could go to NAPO, the National Association of Professional Organizers, which has a huge e-mail list of people who are prequalified to want my bag. I might say to them, "Let's do a partnership where I give a discount to all your members. In return for that discount, you e-mail all your members three times this month about the discount and my products." If they went for that deal, I could instantly increase my database by 500,000 names, as well as my scope of influence and reach. NAPO would be able to give its members something of value to increase their loyalty, and I would get a large e-mail marketing push that would produce sales with new customers. That's a potential cash infusion of a few million dollars that costs me nothing but a phone call.

I've talked about licensing already, and it has the same potential to create cash flow for you. Companies who license your ideas/brands pay you a licensing fee up front along with royalties on sales. That not only creates immediate cash but a steady infusion of new revenue. Strategic partnerships can work the same way. You and a more established partner agree to leverage the partner's marketing budget, customer database, and other resources to sell more of your products, and you split the revenues. The possibilities are limitless.

Control Your Costs

The single most important thing you can do to get through the difficult early financial days is to keep your overhead as low as possible. So many companies throw away thousands and thousands of dollars on things they don't need: professionally designed logos, office space, new computers, advertising campaigns—the list goes on. It is very unlikely that you will need these things in your first year.

Don't grow physically too soon. If you have to grow, you should be bursting at the seams before you do it. If you are thinking about upgrading your office space, make sure that there is no physical way you can fit any longer. Remember that in a lean month, the higher overhead for a larger office could be the difference between making payroll and not. Office space means more than rent. It means insurance, electricity, phone lines, security services, and so on. Use every inch of the space you have before you even think about looking for more.

Here are a few other tips for saving money at the start:

- *Get used equipment.* I'm always surprised when some entrepreneurs recoil at the idea of used computers. Unless you're in a business like animation, in which you've got to have the latest and greatest, a bunch of three-year-old Dells will give you all the computing power you need. You can find used printers, copiers, desks, chairs, and all kinds of other equipment online at sites like SystemsNews.com and UsedBizStuff. com and save hundreds of dollars!
- *Don't hire people you can't afford.* There will be some people whose salary demands are simply beyond what you know you will have. Pass on them. There will be other people. The only indispensable person in your company is you.
- *Hire interns.* They provide free or low-cost work. Interns who work for me learn things they might pay a small fortune for in business school in exchange for their labor. I have interns at my companies all the time. I've hired two of them who are still with me as paid employees.

Don't get caught up in being "showy" and spending more money than you should. Make a "bare essentials" list of the things you need to operate as a business. Anything not on the list you don't get to have. For the things you do need, find out how to get them as cheaply as possible without sacrificing quality. Research your products, and see where you can get them produced and shipped cheapest. See if you can get services in trade—designing someone's logo in exchange for their setting up your network server, for example.

Also, keep in mind that some of the organizations you may join for networking might also offer services at a discount as part of their strategic partnership deal.

Good Debt, Bad Debt

In general, another important part of managing lean times at the start is staying out of debt as much as possible. You hear about entrepreneurs who started their companies by maxing out multiple credit cards, but I can't recommend that method. Sure, you might run up some debt in the beginning, but you should aspire to pay it off as quickly as possible. Think about it this way: if you bought $25,000 in equipment and start-up assets on your credit cards at 15 percent annual interest and could only afford to make the minimum payment each month (a distinct possibility, because you'll likely be strapped for cash), it would take you 431 months to pay off your debt and cost you an extra $31,114 in interest. That's the type of debt that can kill a new company.

It's okay to use credit cards to cover essential expenses as you are launching, but have a plan to pay the debt off within the first twelve months of business. For every successful company started on a mountain of leveraged plastic, I'll bet there are fifty that failed, leaving their founders drowning in red ink with ruined credit. Be careful with this method.

As Jon Hanson, author of *Good Debt, Bad Debt*, says, there is good debt and then there's bad debt. Bad debt wastes money; good debt has the potential to make you money in the long run. In your personal life, good debt would be buying a house at the right time, because it will appreciate. In business, good debt is debt that gives you the opportunity to dramatically grow your business. All debt is a gamble, but one of the skills entrepreneurs develop is the ability to spot an opportunity that offers good odds of paying off with increased sales, incredible publicity, or some other tangible benefit. In those instances, it's worth it to spend some money to make money.

If you have an awesome opportunity to go to Los Angeles and get your fashion products in an Emmy suite, and you know that a bunch of A-list celebrities will be there, that's a calculated risk that's worth taking. You might not have $5,000 for airfare, hotel, rental car, couture, and free samples, so you may have to put it on your credit card, but if the opportunity is too great to pass up, don't let it slip away. That's the type of risk that makes companies into stars. The bump in sales and name recognition that you might get from having your jewelry worn by the cast of a hit TV show or your interior design portfolio seen by the people at HGTV will more than pay for your one-time splurge.

Anyway, it's the ongoing business expenses that you really have to watch. You pay for a lunch here, a new printer there, a working vacation for your staff over there—and boom! Before you know it, you're $10,000 in the hole at a time when business is slow. Then you're in collections, and soon your credit rating is wrecked, and you can't get the capital to run day to day. That kind of thing has killed more than a few companies. Don't let it kill yours.

When you are past the startup phase and are starting to gain market share and economic conditions go downhill, the one thing you should *not* do is decrease your budget for marketing, brand building, and PR. Increase it and all efforts around it. This is counter to conventional wisdom, which is why you should do it. It's the same principle as "buy low, sell high." When the economy is slow and business is slumping, what do most companies do? They cut back on marketing. That means there is more business out there for the taking. Slow times are perfect for aggressive businesses to grab market share. If you have to cut back other expenses during lean periods, make sure you don't chop your business-development budget. A down economy is your best window for a big future when times get better.

Keep It Simple: Do It Yourself

If you're concerned about being able to pay the bills, then "do it yourself" is the way to go. You're already your own best salesperson and best brand builder. For the first twelve months, you'll probably have to be your own administrative assistant, filer, marketing copy-writer, Facebook manager, purchasing agent, project manager, and chief cook and bottle washer. It can make for some long days, but I (and millions of other entrepreneurs) have found that when you're doing what you love, long days don't feel as long. You can learn a lot of skills when the alternative is spending money you don't have. Assume at the outset that you will be working sixteen-hour days six days a week to take care of all the aspects of your business that might later be handled by someone else.

Keep things simple and save. When it's just you and a desk, focus on the fundamentals. Work on establishing a customer base, refining your system of billing and paying bills, polishing your product supply chain, handling customer service issues, working out the bugs in your technology, creating a buzz, and most of all steadily growing your revenue. I didn't launch all my Jen Groover products and services right out of the gate; I put my energy into making the Butler Bag a huge hit first.

For the first six to eight months after launching, plan to spend 80 percent of your time on:

- Branding and public relations
- Sales
- Networking
- Customer service
- Quality control
- Managing vendors

The rest of your time will be eaten up by tasks like paperwork, filing, customizing your office space, setting up your phone service, and all that "housekeeping" work. This way, you're investing most of your valuable time making sure that customers know about and like you, that what you deliver to them is of the best possible quality, and that they have a fantastic experience. There's not much else you need to do to ensure that your company gets off to a fast start.

Dreamer's Corner: A New Entrepreneur Q&A

Claire Loran, Founder
www.egreent.com
claire@egreent.com

1. What is the name of your new business, and when did you start it?

Green T started November 2007.

2. What type of business is it?

I design and sell eco-friendly yoga wear.

3. What was the greatest obstacle you faced in starting your business, and how did you overcome it?

Knowing where to start and how to get everything off the ground. To overcome this I put my many years of business analysis into action—which essentially meant looking at my target goals and working backwards, step by step, until I had worked through all the steps I would need in order to make it happen.

4. What has the experience of being an entrepreneur taught you about yourself, and how has it changed you?

This whole experience has taught me that if you have faith in yourself then you can not only achieve your goals, but often exceed them. I used to be a shy, introverted person with little self-confidence. Taking the leap to become a sole business owner, in an industry that is completely different

(continued)

from my previous career, has been the best thing I have ever done for myself.

5. What is the most important lesson you have learned about starting a business?

There are many:

- Use a good bookkeeper from day one.
- Choose your Web designer and builder carefully. Your website is your virtual storefront, the face of your business that the rest of the world will see, and your biggest branding opportunity.
- Surround yourself with positive, creative people.
- Don't be afraid to make mistakes—just don't make the same mistakes twice.
- Get creative with your marketing. I made the mistake early on of thinking that I needed to have print ads in all the major trade publications. Instead, I have relied on alternatives like local trade shows and festivals, recruiting champions, or ambassadors for my products in key towns and cities.

6. Where is your business today as far as earnings, size, etc.? What are your prospects for the future?

My business today is not yet where I had hoped it to be at this point. The poor economy has definitely had an adverse impact on the company's growth. My client base includes spas, resorts, yoga studios, and boutiques, many of which are under corporate level buying freezes. However, I have used this slow period to build relationships with my buyers, network with other business owners, gain product feedback, develop new and better products, find more cost-effective and creative ways to do business, and build a private label division.

What if all you have to do is make a few adjustments to see profits double?

Sometimes small steps can put a massive charge of profitability into your company. A few years back, a European millionaire decided he wanted to share the lifetime of tips, secrets, and good advice that had helped him become rich by age forty, so he wrote and published a big, glossy book about how to become a millionaire and marketed it around the world. It flopped.

Then he hit on it: **his book was priced too low**. He was selling a book about how to become a millionaire for $50. He realized that since his book was about getting rich, it should feel like a luxury item and be priced accordingly. He increased the price to $1,000 per copy; his sales went from three or four copies a month to two hundred or three hundred. Suddenly, Arab princes and European CEOs had to have a copy of the book; the outrageous price had made it a sought-after status symbol. He hadn't changed a word, and he increased sales by 1,000 percent.

You never know if a few small adjustments in your business model could produce the same kind of leap in sales and profits. That is why it is so tragic when people give up prematurely on their businesses. Sometimes, all that's needed is a price change, a new feature, a fresh logo, or a single story in the press. Very often I see new entrepreneurs selling to one market (the market they had in mind when they started the company) even though their true market is slightly different. Sometimes you don't know who really wants your product until you're out in the market and you discover who *doesn't* want it.

This has happened to us often with the Butler Bag. When I launched I had one idea about who my target market was but what I quickly realized was we had extremely loyal customers in categories we never thought of. For example, we quickly learned that we had a die-hard consumer group of knitters. I have never knitted so it wasn't a market I'd ever thought of, but once we realized that, we focused marketing efforts toward that demographic and built on what had already occurred organically.

Look at Beanie Babies. Ty Warner, the founder of Ty Inc. and creator of the toys, developed the little beanbag dolls for kids, but he soon found that adults were collecting them madly, and he started rolling out new dolls as quickly as possible to fuel the collecting mania. By the 1990s the plush critters had grown into a monster fad perpetuated by grown-ups, and Ty was a multimillionaire. That's what can happen if you find out that your market isn't what you thought it was and turn that surprise into an opportunity.

Think ahead about small tweaks you can make to your pricing, marketing, sales, customer service, networking, website, billing, and so on. Consider these points also:

- Price your products or services appropriately. One of the most common problems I see is entrepreneurs who under-price what they are selling. Fight that tendency, and ask for the higher price. Most of the time, you'll be pleasantly surprised that customers won't even blink at a price you thought was too high.

- Consider creating artificial scarcity. Disney has created incredible ongoing demand for its library of movies by releasing just a few classics at a time for a short period and then putting them back into the vault. That's smart. When something is harder to get, people want it more. I have never made it easy for customers to get my high-end bags; they have to go to upscale boutiques. Think about how you can apply the principle of scarcity to your business model.

- Collaborate with some of your best customers on your marketing to give it new creative life. Visit their offices and invite each CEO to be your creative director for a day, sharing what they see as the strongest and weakest points of your branding and marketing. Then put the advice into action.

- Form a partnership with a popular charity in your area, dedicating a certain percentage of your sales, or all your sales for one day per month, to that charity. The resulting positive PR will be priceless.

- If you don't already, start offering a 100 percent satisfaction guarantee. This is unusual if you're in a service business, but that's what makes it powerful. Offer clients their money back if they are not completely satisfied with your work. Typically, a very small percentage of people will ever ask for their money back, but the guarantee makes you look supremely confident in the quality of your service.

- Give it six months before you start making changes, unless the need for changes becomes obvious. Every business needs time to catch on and get its footing. If you make changes too quickly, you could alienate customers. Remember, it's a marathon, not a hundred-meter dash. Make sure your eyes and ears are always open and that you are taking notes.

Why not continually improve every aspect of your business?

Previously I mentioned creative destruction. There's a similar principle that I love: *kaizen*. It's the Japanese word for "improvement," and Toyota has turned it into a market-defining strategy. Basically, what makes Toyota such an incredible company is that it is always breaking down and reinventing its business model from the ground up. Nothing is sacred, so nothing gets stale. The company never rests on its laurels because it is always looking for new ways to cut costs, reduce the time it takes to build a car, and improve quality.

There's a reason that Toyota has become the most successful car brand in the world: *kaizen*.

Rather than wait to make adjustments to your business model after you see that it's not working, why not constantly make small changes so that you're always finding new ways to improve? Try *split-testing strategies,* by which you can test different sales and marketing strategies at the same time in similar conditions. This lets you compare the results and constantly gauge which method is working better. Also, every week, you could sit down, look back at the activity of the previous week, and figure out small ways you can do things better. Maybe one week you realize that documents you e-mailed to a client as a PDF would be better delivered by hand so you could have personal contact. Another week you might figure out a way to make the navigation of your website simpler. Each small change adds up, and over time you will enhance your business model and solve problems before they happen.

When launching a company entrepreneurs are always so busy looking forward, we often forget how powerful it is to look back and reflect. Make sure this doesn't happen to you!

What if
your idea is so strong that your business explodes overnight?

Sometimes a business idea becomes like an avalanche. All you can do is hang on, build an infrastructure on the fly, and enjoy the ride. That's a situation most entrepreneurs would be happy to find themselves in, because the momentum gives you so many opportunities to learn and grow. Seeing an idea catch fire is such a joyous and energizing experience that tasks you used to dread—like doing the books or doing interviews with the news media—suddenly become fun and exciting. When you're riding a wave of passion, the learning curve doesn't seem so steep anymore.

Back in 2001, Lisa Druxman wanted to spend more time with her newborn child and still remain fit, so instead of going back to her job managing a high-end gym, she launched a simple idea: Stroller Strides, fitness classes for busy moms in her San Diego County neighborhood. Simple idea, simple execution. But it filled a huge unmet need: fitness for busy moms who could take their strollers along on their workouts. When one of her local instructors relocated and suggested that Lisa let her test-market the concept in her new city, moms went wild. Today, Lisa has more than one hundred Stroller Stride franchisees (it's one of the fastest-growing franchises in the country), sells custom strollers, and has written her own book on fitness for moms. All from a simple neighborhood mommy class!

Many successful businesses don't even start out as businesses— just personal projects. Momar Taal was a university student when he and some friends started designing and printing T-shirts that represented their own personal style and personality. "All of a sudden we were printing custom orders for friends, and before you knew it we were printing for nearly everyone we knew," he said in an interview for the BizLaunch small business blog. "We recognized a unique opportunity for our style of clothing and the message it represented. So we began designing and people started to recognize and connect with our vision. That's when we discovered our passion. We started focusing on branding and marketing and everything took off from there." The resulting company, Malyka, has become a phenomenon, with stores in North America and the Caribbean.

There is no way to know if your idea will catch lightning in a bottle like these. Increase your odds by:

- Keeping it simple
- Making sure you're totally passionate about your idea
- Finding a need that's not being met and filling it
- Creating media and online buzz

- Delivering value in a way that's different from what everyone else is doing

If you are lucky enough to have your business idea take off like a rocket, stay true to your vision while being prepared to adapt, create relationships with potential business allies who are suddenly eager to meet you, find financial and legal advisors you can trust, don't say no to publicity opportunities even if they seem insignificant (they could lead to great things), and enjoy the profitability while it lasts!

What if *after six lean months, you make more money than you ever dreamed of?*

Fear of financial ruin is the most common obstacle for people who are still on the fence about starting their companies. But what they don't ask is, "What if I hit it big?" It does happen. After the initial ramp-up period, you could become a huge hit. After a rough first year filled with manufacturing snafus and red ink, my company took off and, after four years, is quickly becoming one of the most robust lifestyle accessory brands. So it is possible to bypass the long, lonely highway of scraping by and eating ramen noodles and go straight to the Having the Life of Your Dreams exit.

Nobody can predict what new businesses will make a huge splash and massive profits right out of the gate; anyone who says he can is fooling himself and you. However, fast-starting and profitable new businesses tend to have a few elements in common:

- *A unique, memorable brand.* Branding is the difference maker for any company, and having a brand that's known, appealing, and consistent will attract many new customers to you without any effort on your part.

- *Great word of mouth.* Personal testimonials are the greatest advertising, and fast-rising companies frequently rise—especially in the age of the internet—because lots of people are raving about how wonderful they are.
- *Endless hard work.* The old saying "The harder I work, the luckier I get" is absolutely true. Entrepreneurs who are willing to put in the long hours at the start to get a business up and running are usually the ones who make the big profits faster. They are refining their business model, networking, developing new products or services, and finding better ways to solve problems.
- *Innovation.* If you start the one thousandth version of a consulting business, you'll become just another consultant in the minds of clients. But if you put a new wrinkle in your business, you become something more. What if you self-published a book on your consulting ideas before you ever hung out your shingle? Originality fuels success.
- *Opportunism.* Great entrepreneurs keep their ears to the ground and are aware of everything that's going on in their industry—and with others as well. When a new opportunity first appears like the first shoot of a spring flower, they're on it aggressively. They're the first to pop up with a new proposal or to make a vital phone call.

Why not start locally?

Another way to improve your odds of being profitable right out of the gate is to limit your launch to your local community. This way, you become a big fish in a small pond. It's not always best to get too big too fast. If you're worried about the costs of doing business nationally or even globally, then at launch, just do business in your home city or metropolitan area. If you live in a big enough region—like the Philadelphia/New York City area where I do most of my work—you may never need to expand beyond your local space. There are more than enough customers in New York City alone to make almost any small business prosperous.

Think of all the ways you can save money by focusing for your first twelve months on doing business within a fifty-mile radius of your home office (especially if you're a product-based business):

- Instead of paying a fortune to ship products all over the country, you could get a fuel-efficient car and handle deliveries personally. This also gives you a chance to meet your customers face-to-face.
- Client meetings cost next to nothing because you're not flying or staying in hotels.
- Rather than hiring a publicist to get press coverage, you could handle it yourself by building rapport with your local media. You'll probably have better odds of being covered because you're a hometown business. This is the "local celebrity" strategy I talk about in Chapter 7.
- By building local relationships, you can get discounts on advertising, connect with local charities, and find sponsorship opportunities.

Of course, you should always remain receptive to and aware of opportunities on a larger—national or global—scale. You certainly don't want to lock yourself into a local-only mode and turn down what could be a life-changing account or partnership from a company in another time zone. But those things will take care of themselves. Control costs at the beginning by controlling the size of your market, and expand in a controlled, gradual way. It's far easier to create hot buzz, go viral, and build a winning brand when you're focusing your attention and resources.

Why not talk to a banker about tactics like borrowing against your receivables?

The above ideas sound great, but then there are those first six months to survive. That's where this advice helps. Cash flow is an issue for almost every company. That's why the credit freeze of 2009 was such a blow to the economy. Many companies borrow in the short term to make their expenses because customers take thirty, sixty, and ninety days to pay their bills. Now that the credit market is starting to ease, you can do the same thing if you have a lot of sales but not a lot of cash coming in because you're waiting to get paid.

Many banks, especially small, community business banks, will do what's called "accounts receivable lending" (also known as "factoring"). Basically, you're borrowing money from the bank and using the value of your accounts receivable as collateral. With most of these programs, you essentially sell your receivables to the bank for less than they are worth, and the bank takes over collections, getting the additional cash when (or if) they collect. In return, you get cash that you can use to make payroll (if you have employees), fund expansion, or pay for manufacturing. You can learn more about factoring at these sites:

- InvestorWords.com
- Toolkit.com
- BusinessDictionary.com

Banks might ask you to sell your receivables for as much as 5 percent less than what they are worth (or in rare cases even more), so if you have $20,000 owed to you, you might only get $19,000 for it. Over a year or more, the cost of selling your receivables in this way might be greater than getting a traditional loan. So this is not something you want to do regularly. However, it can be a godsend when you're just starting out—if you have a robust customer base, a lot of receivables due in less than ninety days, and a bank you can trust. Be careful with this option, but look at it as a way of taking advantage of the fact that you're great at making the sale but have no control over when your customers will cut you a check.

Lessons Learned

- ► Fears of not being able to pay the bills are usually greater than the reality.
- ► Ensuring that you get paid before you have to pay others is a critical part of managing cash flow.
- ► Cash infusion is the lifeblood of your business; get creative and diversify your revenue streams.
- ► There are many ways to infuse your company with cash, including new opportunities, licensing, and partnerships.
- ► Debt that gives you the chance to grow and profit is worth taking on.
- ► Keeping things as simple as possible and doing as much as you can yourself in the beginning can keep costs down.
- ► There's no rule that says you won't make money right away.
- ► Doing business locally can reduce your costs.
- ► Small adjustments in your business plan can sometimes yield huge profit increases.
- ► Borrowing against your accounts receivable is another option for generating immediate capital.

The Next Twenty-Four

In the next twenty-four hours . . .

✓ Brainstorm ways you could infuse cash into your business when you need it.

✓ List opportunities that might be worth taking on some debt, and list how much debt.

✓ List the things you could do yourself for your company and how many hours they would likely take each week.

✓ Write down ways you might tweak your business in midstream to boost your profitability.

✓ Identify at least three community business banks with good reputations that could be trustworthy sources of accounts receivable loans.

My Dream Plan, Part 9

Outline your launch strategy.

Ways I will minimize costs at launch:

_____

_____

_____

_____

Possible methods of infusing cash into my business:

_____

_____

_____

_____

How I will generate press coverage at launch:

_____

_____

_____

_____

Key relationships I will focus on creating:

_____

_____

_____

_____

My first sales targets:

_____

_____

_____

_____

10

"What if I fail?"

> *Do not be too timid and squeamish about your actions. All life is an experiment. The more experiments you make the better. What if they are a little coarse, and you may get your coat soiled or torn? What if you do fail, and get fairly rolled in the dirt once or twice? Up again, you shall never be so afraid of a tumble.*
>
> —Ralph Waldo Emerson

This is the Big Kahuna of entrepreneur obstacles: self-doubt. One of my mantras is "Have more fear of regret than failure," but most people seem to worry more about how they will see themselves in the mirror if they take that big leap and fall flat on their faces. I would wager that fear of failure has stopped more would-be successful new companies than lack of funding, economic downturns, and competition all put together.

They don't teach you a thing in business school about how to handle those dark-night-of-the-soul doubts and fears, which to me is one more reason not to worry about business school. You're either going to learn how to overcome your fears on the street in the real world getting things done, or you're not. Malcolm Forbes said, "When you cease to dream, you cease to live." I want you to achieve all of your dreams. So let's talk about some of the strategies I've used for handling the fear of failure and how you can turn them into your own.

Remember that when I was a kid I was terrified to look bad in front of my peers. What I didn't tell you was that I quit my TV job because I was afraid that every time I flubbed a line, people watching would laugh at me. My self-esteem at the time was not strong enough to handle that. I had to develop a strong sense of self to be able to be at the center of a whirl of businesses. It's the same with a professional athlete or an entertainer: everything revolves around you, like it or not. You have to develop an impenetrable sense of who you are and what you're worth to be able to direct others and be the center of the activity. If I hadn't been able to do that, I wouldn't have lasted a year in business, because I am essentially the brand.

My organization is not a traditional hierarchy. It's me in the center with lots of partners and projects. The number of employees fluctuates depending on the projects but usually is between ten and twenty. Managing those people and still having time for my creativity is very challenging, but I learned an important lesson early on. I had a hard time keeping my hands off aspects of the business that weren't a good use of my time. Entrepreneurs love opportunities, so often we try to take on too much for fear of missing out on something. In the beginning, I wanted people to know I was in the trenches, too, working as hard or harder than they were. I thought that if they didn't see me working, they wouldn't respect me; they would figure I was delegating and not really doing. I didn't have a strong enough sense of my worth, even though I had built the company! I had a real "come to Jesus" moment about this. When we would get a shipment in—boxes and boxes of bags—I would be carrying boxes into the warehouse with my team! Me, the CEO! Finally, one day I thought, "What am I doing? This is not a good use of my time! I should be on the phone making deals happen!" It struck me clearly that the best and highest use of my talents was as the brand and the creator of new opportunities.

The first time I didn't tote that barge and lift that bale, one of my employees challenged me on it. What I learned at that moment was that although you do want your people to see you working as hard as they are, you don't want them to see you on their level if you are their leader. These were people whose checks I was signing every week. I called a meeting and asked, "Would you rather me carry boxes in or be on the phone getting them sold? If we get them into the warehouse and they stay there, then no one has a job." Silence. Everyone knew the answer. If I hadn't developed a strong sense of self and of my worth as a leader and entrepreneur, I might have wilted before the challenge from that employee. I became more of a leader at that moment.

Failure Isn't Personal

You will fail in your business. It may be a small setback or a major hurdle, or it may kill your business. You know what? You can and will bounce back if you do one thing:

Don't take failure as a judgment of your character or ability.

Failure happens for a huge range of reasons. Sometimes the market simply isn't ready for an innovation, which is what happened during the first wave of e-commerce back in the late 1990s. Internet connections were too slow, too few people were buying things online, and the business models were still being worked out. But today, e-commerce is a multibillion-dollar behemoth. The EV1, the electric car from General Motors, is another example. People who leased the cars loved them, but the car really was a clunker with poor range and performance. The battery technology just hadn't come far enough yet, and GM killed the project.

Some of the other reasons that businesses fail include:

- Competitors are just too entrenched.
- A competitor comes up with a product or service that devours the lion's share of the business in that market, like Windows.
- Funding dries up, and a new source can't be found.
- A major cultural shift changes business conditions. For example, several airlines went belly-up after 9/11, but that wasn't their fault. People weren't flying.
- Government subsidies get cancelled.
- The economy plunges into recession.

And yes, sometimes businesses crash because their founders make fatal errors or delude themselves into thinking there is a market for their product when there isn't. We all have to guard against self-delusion. We have to be realistic and ask ourselves if we're trying to force something on buyers that they don't want or need. If we decide that is the case, we have to be wise and disciplined enough to move on to the next idea. But in every one of those reasons, there's nothing personal.

When you take a risk, you risk failure. When you step into the spotlight with a new idea, you risk that someone will reach out from the side of the stage with that big hook. It doesn't mean you're not fit to be an entrepreneur or that you'll never come up with an idea that will make you a good living and make the world a better place. It means one thing: **this idea didn't work this time**.

The Wrong Question

When I counsel new entrepreneurs—especially people who have already tried to make an idea work and watched it fall flat—I find that they are gun-shy about getting back on the horse. If their self-esteem was shaky before, it's as fragile as spun glass after one business failure. They'll ask me, "Jen, what if I try again and fail again?" I reply, "That's the wrong question. The question you should be asking is, 'What did I learn from this last experience that's going to help my next idea be a huge success?'" After all, failure is life's greatest teacher. As I mentioned previously, there is not one successful entrepreneur I have met who hasn't failed. It is in their failures that they find success. Failure is an incredible opportunity to learn and grow; it's a means to an end. It's not the end in itself.

It is far better to focus on dealing with what happens when you succeed. Success brings its own challenges. What will you do for an encore? How will it impact your time? Those are great problems to have! Thinking about the success you're going to experience is very liberating. Another thing I say to people is, "Wow, that was a great failure! You probably learned a hell of a lot!" You should see how that rocks them backward. They had not thought of failure that way because they were so busy beating themselves up personally because of it.

If you launch a company and it craters after a year, you're not the same person as when you started. You've gained tremendous experience and knowledge and wisdom, and in that you have not failed. You also know what doesn't work, and you're closer to figuring out what does. Every day you are going to have failures and think, "God, that was so dumb!" I've done that many times. There are people I shouldn't have hired and deals I shouldn't have made. I look back now and wonder why someone didn't try to talk me out of some of those decisions. But no one could have done that. I had to make those mistakes because that was the only way I was going to learn. The aggravation that I caused my company was more than worth it. With every failure there comes (like a sort of secret toy surprise in the bottom of the cereal box) added value in strength, wisdom, and knowledge.

Transforming Your Mind

If you're going to overcome the fear of failure and become a success as an entrepreneur, you must transform the way you think. I constantly have to do this to dodge negative vibes in daily business. I have to shift my energy. If I sense frustration creeping into my emotions, then I go find something or someone who can help me shift the energy. Having people in your circle who can shift your thinking from the negative to the positive is very important. What you don't want to do is call on people who will expand that negativity by talking about all the bad things that might happen.

This discipline is all about knowing how your mind works and how to manage your thoughts. A huge part of the entrepreneur's journey is self-awareness. Self-actualization breeds successful entrepreneurs. Entrepreneurship becomes a spiritual calling, not just a financial or economic calling. You find yourself questioning what makes reality: something outside you or your thoughts? How do you need to adjust your thinking to retain the momentum you've built up? It's scary, but you have control.

For me, music is a wonderful tool for controlling mood and staying in a positive frame of mind. Many mornings, I play "Right Now" by Van Halen when I am getting ready to begin my day; it gets me in a mind space where I feel like I can take on the world! Music can shift your mind-set almost instantly. Discover the tricks that work to keep you positive and motivated.

It's also important to expect the best but have the skill set to handle the worst. Go for the great outcome, but become the kind of person who can handle it when things go wrong. I'm good at thinking on my feet. You also need to be resilient and resourceful, not take obstacles personally, and truly believe that you can turn any situation around. I don't waste time on hypothetical situations. I have too much positive, forward-motion thinking to do.

If your mind-set is not right and you are not constantly monitoring and controlling it, you will cave in before the first trouble that comes at you. That would be a waste. Entrepreneurs change the world. Thomas Edison, Ben Franklin—they transformed civilization. What we do is noble. It's bigger than a road map to success. It's about shifting your perspective and living your life with the mind-set that you can change everything—that you are significant, not just successful. Being an entrepreneur is about becoming a different person and inspiring and touching other lives on the journey. You're in the position to work on yourself every day. You have to stare at yourself every day and face down your weaknesses. You must transform yourself into someone who embodies the best qualities of the company you want to build—then you can build that company.

These days, when I get the sensation in my stomach of being uncomfortable, I'm exhilarated. I know that I'm on a one-way street out of my comfort zone and that it always leads to something great. Remember how my mother said, "If you weren't uncomfortable today, you didn't grow today"? My follow-up is, "Once you do something that makes you uncomfortable, you will never be the same again."

Who do you want to become? First, change yourself. Who are you supposed to be? Start there. Everything else falls into place.

Dreamer's Corner: A New Entrepreneur Q&A

Alexandra Leikermoser, Founder
www.yogagurl.com
click@yogagurl.com

1. What is the name of your new business, and when did you start it?

Yogagurl grew organically after my burnout as an eco-designer. It started as a passion in 2001 and over the last eight years has grown into a business.

2. What type of business is it?

A yoga line of clothing with cheeky sayings and layers, as well as inspirational products. The second component of the business is offering on-site yoga for events and corporations.

3. What was the greatest obstacle you faced in starting your business, and how did you overcome it?

I started my first business at twenty-five years old. At thirty years old I was an eco–interior designer. I had five dollars in my pocket, was diagnosed with chronic fatigue, and knew I had to make changes in the way I ran business and my health. A friend paid for my yoga teacher training course. I did not know where taking time off would lead me. That was eight years ago.

During my yoga training I was in a car accident, which added to the urgency of making changes in my life as an entrepreneur. It made me seriously look at my health, life, and where I wanted to go. I think my health was the biggest obstacle.

4. What has the experience of being an entrepreneur taught you about yourself, and how has it changed you?

Being an entrepreneur all my life has forced me to be creative with challenges that come my way. To always have to create your own income forces you to be accountable for your decisions. It has also taught me to

224

take risks and go outside of my comfort zone. It has made me recognize my unique gifts and how to manage and delegate in order to find happiness, balance, health, and wealth in my life!

5. What is the most important lesson you have learned about starting a business?

Follow your passion and always believe in yourself. Don't listen to others when they say something is not possible! Following your heart will always take you on the path of success.

6. Where is your business today as far as earnings, size, etc.? What are your prospects for the future?

I have downsized my company to become more virtual and simplify my life. My business was selling my clothing line in Los Angeles and New York to top stores such as Equinox Fitness. I hit a wall in terms of my health again last year, and I experienced exponential growth that was beyond my business knowledge to handle. I did not have the proper mentors and physical energy to take it to the next level and was not sure that was what I wanted. The future holds amazing possibilities. By taking a year off to reassess and recharge, I now have a clearer picture of my strengths and weaknesses and where I want to go! I am writing a book about yoga health and business, speaking at conferences for women, and looking at licensing my products and services.

Whine Less, Breathe More . . .

What if you succeed?

When I hear novice business launchers asking, "But what if I fail?" I immediately turn the idea around and ask, "But what if you succeed?" We've been taught to think that optimism is irresponsible and that wisdom means acknowledging all the things that can go wrong. That's why some people seem to spend so much time prophesying doom and gloom: they think it makes them look wise. Someone who focuses on the good things that can happen is a Pollyanna—until things do go right. Then everyone says, "I knew it all along!"

No one should take risks expecting to fail. Why launch your company if you're not expecting to succeed? So when you find yourself thinking negatively, try dwelling on what could happen if you actually do succeed. New companies launch every week and last for twenty, thirty, or forty years, sometimes being bought for millions by larger corporations, sometimes becoming big public corporations themselves, and often remaining small, thriving businesses that are passed down through families. What a splendid legacy.

But think about something else as well: what does success mean in your dictionary? It's different for everyone. My idea of a successful business venture is not going to be the same as yours or anyone else's. Everyone wants something unique out of his or her entrepreneurial adventure. You need to know what constitutes success for you so that when you're running your business, you have something to aim for. These are some of the very different ways I have heard entrepreneurs describe success:

- Making enough money to live a comfortable lifestyle while doing what I love everyday
- Making twice what I made at my last job
- Being independent and never having to depend on an employer
- Having no debt
- Having a million-dollar net worth
- Earning enough to retire at age fifty and sail the South Pacific
- Waking up every day stimulated and excited to be alive
- Creating at least one hundred new jobs

- Working at home and raising my kids
- Turning my ideas into realities and getting paid for it
- Making the world a better place
- Inspiring others to want more for their lives and strive to live up to their human potential
- Becoming the best person I can be

Notice that there's not much there about being a mogul or taking a company public and becoming a billionaire. There's nothing wrong with either one, of course, but the point is that entrepreneurship is supposed to fuel your dream lifestyle. Whatever kind of life would bring you joy—being at home with your kids, traveling constantly to great foreign cities, helping boost the local economy, inventing things—that's the kind of success you should design your business for. If you love nothing more than being at home with your family and working from a cozy home office, why would you create a company that required you to be on the road for two hundred days a year? You would be miserable!

So when you are tempted to dwell on the possibility of failure, practice turning that idea on its head, and focus your attention on the *probability* of success. Then think about what kind of success you want to bring into being, because it won't just happen. *You* have to make your perfect life come true.

What if you spend the rest of your life regretting not taking the chance?

Hockey immortal Wayne Gretzky said, "You'll always miss 100 percent of the shots you don't take." You may regret not talking to the pretty girl in high school, not trying out for the team because you were afraid of looking foolish, and not starting your dream company because you worried you would not be able to pay the mortgage. If you don't at least try to turn your vision into a business—if you always play it safe—how will you feel about yourself in ten years? Will you beat yourself up because you had a brief window to at least give it a try and to test yourself? More often than not, I believe the answer to that question will be yes!

In the United States, we live in a world largely without opportunities to test ourselves and build our character. The life of even impoverished people in this country today is a walk in the park compared to the life of a pioneer settler or a frontier soldier two hundred years ago. In those days, we didn't have to seek out ways to test our mettle, will, or strength; they came to us in the form of wars, native tribes, and natural disasters. But today, we live in a world stripped of chances to find out what we're made of. That's why we create events like the Ultraman (a double triathlon), why sailors race single-handedly and nonstop around the world, and why people still climb Mount Everest. Human beings crave the opportunity to push their limits.

Starting a business will test you. You're pitting your wits and dedication against an indifferent world, competitors who want to crush you, and creditors who are going to keep sending you bills whether or not you can pay them. It's a test of who you are and what you've got inside. Some people thrive on this sort of adrenaline rush, which is why after they create one company and sell it, they go on and create more. I thrive on it, or I wouldn't do what I do. You'll never know if you thrive on the thrill and challenge of business unless you take a risk and do it. It will change who you are and how you live, and even if you fail, you will be able to say, "I gave it my best!"

What if this idea doesn't work out but it inspires an even better one?

Okay, so your first big idea was a flop. Fine. It happens. So what? Odds are that you learned more about business in the three or six or twelve months it took for your idea to go bust than you did in the last five years. More to the point, your failed idea probably revealed flaws, openings, and opportunities in the market that might lead you to launch something a hundred times better. That's a failure worth having in my book. Sometimes you don't know what works until you figure out what *doesn't* work.

It happens all the time. Dean Kamen, the brilliant inventor who is most famous for the Segway personal transport but who has changed the world with his medical devices and cheap water purifier, says that he can't even count all his failures. In an interview given in January 2009 for the Business Opportunities Weblog Network, he said of inventors and failure, "It's not that [inventors are] brilliant or well-educated. They work all the time. They don't let failure demoralize or destroy them. They pick themselves up and keep going and eventually, every once in a while, one of your ideas actually breaks through and works, and it makes all that stuff seem worthwhile."

There are many ways you're likely to get new ideas from a failed one. Let's say you're launching and marketing a new online social network aimed at a niche audience like reality TV watchers. You launch it, it teeters on the brink for a year, and then advertising falls off, and you have to shut down. Cue the sad music. But what did you discover during that failure? You probably got ideas for online features that would work well on other websites, met possible partners, discovered new facts about your target market, and a lot more. Your failure probably led to at least five potential new business ideas, any one of which could turn out to be a blockbuster. This is the evolutionary process of great entrepreneurs.

One failure leads to multiple inspirations. That's how it worked for the scientists at NASA and for the Wright brothers. They were creating new technologies out of thin air, a process that's notoriously hit or miss. But what would have happened if they had given up after one model aircraft crashed or one rocket blew up on the pad at Cape Canaveral? Granted, someone would have eventually invented the airplane, and the Soviet Union would have ended up on the moon, but it might have taken years longer and set society back who knows how far.

Why not interview ten successful entrepreneurs and ask them how their failures led to success?

Nothing inspires like knowing someone did exactly the same things you did, felt exactly the same fears you felt, and succeeded wildly anyway. That's why stories of people coming back from injuries to mountain climb, cycle, or play football again are so inspiring. That's what has made Lance Armstrong a hero. We see people facing pain and frustration and going on to success, and we think, "If they can do it, so can I!"

That's why I strongly encourage you to become part journalist in your journey to becoming an entrepreneur. Help yourself stay focused on success by talking to people who have overcome the odds to succeed. They don't have to be in your industry; the lessons are universal. Start making contact with the most successful professionals you know and asking to interview them. Take notes or record what they say, and find out how they failed on their road to ultimate triumph. You can be certain that every one of them has experienced failure, loss, despair, betrayal, and the overwhelming desire to quit. But somehow, they got through it and became wiser and stronger. Ask:

- What advice would you give an entrepreneur who's just getting started?
- What was your greatest failure, and what did you learn from it?
- Did you learn more from a formal education or from doing business?
- What are the three most valuable lessons you've picked up?
- How did failures make your current success possible?
- How do you get past a negative mind-set?

People love to share their stories, and you'll be amazed at the volume and quality of knowledge you will get. You'll get a master class in real-world business—Street Smarts 101—with each interview. It could be the most valuable resource you ever have for overcoming difficulty and making your business dreams into reality.

If you do not have access to some of the people who intrigue you, see if they have written a book or have a speaking engagement you can attend. I'm sure they will share some of the answers to your questions in stories about their personal journey.

Why not preserve the most valuable lessons from every up and down of your business experience?

We've talked about the unsurpassed education you get from the hard knocks of business. But how do you hold on to those lessons? Some will stay in your brain as if they were burned in with a branding iron, but what about the ones that don't? There's a simple answer: record every lesson you learn from your life as an entrepreneur, no matter how trivial it may seem at the time. You can do this by logging your experiences daily in a handwritten business lesson journal or using a digital voice recorder to capture your impressions and thoughts.

You could also go to Blogger.com, TypePad.com, or WordPress.com and start a blog for free in which you write about all the things you learn the hard way from being in business. I love the blogging idea because it's so open and raw and invites other people to really get to know you and your brand. There are probably other ways to create a business lesson journal that I haven't even considered. Do what works for you.

In essence, you're creating a business education library that lets you go back and review the decisions you made, bits of wisdom you picked up, mistakes to avoid, and great ideas you vowed to come back to. It might even become the content for your book someday! If your journal is physical, then you might even save things like memos, printed copies of e-mails, and other artifacts to jog your memory. The following are some things to consider archiving.

- Mistakes and why you made them
- Things you didn't know before you got into business
- Meaningful statements that people have made to you
- Innovative, wild, or crazy ideas
- Business tips
- Reminders of how you want to modify your own behavior

Every so often, go back and review the material you've set down to see what it can teach you. Do this even when you don't have a problem or hit a business roadblock. But especially when things aren't going well, sift through your collected wisdom for some answers. You might find a new idea, a way of solving a problem, or the name of a potential mentor in those pages, Web postings, or audio files. You never know.

Why not .... get accountability partners to keep you motivated?

Everybody in any business needs some accountability partners. These are colleagues or friends who are willing to hold you responsible for your promises and give you a swift kick in the backside whenever you start to fall short of the achievements you've promised to yourself. I have them; so does every successful entrepreneur I know of. Why? Because we're all human. We all fall short of our intentions and expectations from time to time. If commitment always led to performance, people wouldn't need personal trainers. Having someone to nag, encourage, and push you is critical, especially when business is stressful and you're tempted to phone it in.

Who could your accountability partners be? How about colleagues who also have their own businesses? Friends are fine as long as they are not such good friends that they won't be 100 percent honest with you. A great accountability partner is part drill sergeant, part football coach, and part therapist. He or she has to know when to be gentle and give a pat on the back and when you need a candid, no-nonsense boot to another part of your anatomy.

Here's how to make the most of accountability partners:

- *Start a group, and be each other's partners.* This way, your accountability discipline also becomes a source for networking and new ideas.
- *Set the ground rules.* Each member of your accountability group will want different things from his or her partners, so establish those guidelines early. For yourself, how do you want to be contacted? By phone, e-mail, Twitter, or in person? Are any areas of your life or business off-limits?
- *Write down goals and commitments.* Talk is cheap. Writing everything down gives your accountability partners

something to hold over your head when you need somebody to crack the whip.

- *Have regular meetings with your partners.* Get together every week, and talk about what you've done, how close you are to goals, and where you've fallen short. Compare notes, and make commitments about what you'll do before the next meeting.

- *Establish penalties for not reaching certain goals.* These should be good-natured, because you're already paying a penalty in your business. But sanctions like not taking everyone in the group to dinner for not reaching your sales goal for the month adds consequences and reinforces the fact that your accountability buddies are there to push you to be better.

Lessons Learned

- ► Fear of failure stops more businesses than any other factor.
- ► Fear of failure is largely a result of a deficit of self-worth, not feeling that you have what it takes to succeed, or fear of ridicule if you do not meet your goals.
- ► Failure is not a judgment of your character or ability; sometimes things just happen.
- ► Failure can be something to cherish when it means you really stepped far out on a limb.
- ► Much of success lies in transforming your mind to block negativity.
- ► You could succeed. It happens.
- ► Your failure could inspire an even greater triumph.
- ► Business is much easier with accountability partners and a brain trust helping you out.

The Next Twenty-Four

In the next twenty-four hours . . .

✓ Write down the things you fear and the things that excite
you about pursuing your vision.

✓ Check off the qualities from my Entrepreneur Self-Test
(below) that match you.

✓ Describe what success would be for you.

✓ List people who might become accountability buddies.

✓ List successful entrepreneurs you could talk to about
their failures.

✓ Make a promise to yourself to take enough of a risk to
have one grand, spectacular failure.

Being an entrepreneur is a lifestyle. It's an all-encompassing way
of life. My friends who are entrepreneurs all live very fulfilled lives.
They are living in their passion and doing what they love and controlling their destinies. Even when they fail or struggle financially,
they love the lives they have created. I think that is why so many
millions of people crave the same lifestyle even with its challenges,
ups, and downs. They know that being able to use their creativity to
build something, watch their dreams turn into reality, and be independent is a wonderful way to live.

Some people ask me, "Jen, am I an entrepreneur?" I smile when
I hear that, because almost everyone, given encouragement and
inspiration, can be an entrepreneur. Are you unsure if you're an
entrepreneur? Try this on for size:

Jen's Entrepreneur Self-Test
---

1. Do you have a passion about something and want to change the world with it?
2. Do you see problems and start thinking of ways to solve them?
3. Are you the one who leads all the teams, clubs, or projects?
4. Do you love being creative?
5. Do you see opportunities where others don't?
6. Are you always writing down your ideas?
7. Has anyone ever told you that an idea of yours was crazy and would never work?
8. Do you dream of a life in which you can do things your way and have more control over your future?
9. Do you take failure not as an end but as a classroom?
10. Do you see tough times as chances to grow?

How many of those statements fit you? I'll bet more than a few. Did the results surprise you? They surprise most people, because everyone is caught up in worries about funding and business experience and having an MBA. The most vital ingredients for any entrepreneur are heart, drive, and the ability to see things that don't exist yet and make them reality.

Seeing yourself as an entrepreneur is the first step to becoming one. Admitting that you have what it takes may be the boost that gets you past the first hurdle, which is starting your company. They say adversity reveals your character, and I think starting a business is the act of inviting adversity into your world. So you could say that *entrepreneurship* reveals your character. How will you know what you can do unless you get out there and try?

My Dream Plan, Part 10

Outline how you will handle your fears.

My greatest fear about launching my business:

_____

_____

_____

_____

How I will channel that fear into something positive:

_____

_____

_____

_____

My plan for making the most of failure:

_____

_____

_____

_____

How I hope launching my business will change me:

_____

_____

_____

_____

My launch date:

_____

Stay in Touch!

I hope as you go forward you will e-mail me at jen@whatifand-whynot.com with your successes, failures, questions, and ideas. I would love to know them. And don't forget to send me your Dream Plan at the same address. Hopefully one day I'll be reading *your* book.

Jen Groover

Tagged by *Success* magazine as a "One-Woman Brand" and "Creativity and Innovation Guru," a leading "Serial Entrepreneur" by *Entrepreneur* magazine, and having drawn comparisons to Walt Disney and Benjamin Franklin, Jen Groover's name has quickly become synonymous with innovation, entrepreneurship, and evolution. This concept and product development expert has not only masterminded and built her own companies but has also assisted in the launch of more than fifty other companies. She has gone from guest-hosting spots on QVC to inking deals with some of the industry's biggest heavyweights.

Although it was Jen's innovative handbag company (the award-winning Butler Bag Company, which launched just under three years ago and is now being tracked as one of the fastest-growing handbag brands in history) that catapulted her into the spotlight, her experience, appeal, and expertise extend far beyond the fashion industry. With a vast breadth of sharp, relevant knowledge on everything from business issues to education to government policy and with a natural, energetic on-air presence, Jen is a force to be reckoned with. Jen and her products have been featured in hundreds of media outlets such as *O, The Oprah Magazine*, *Redbook*, *Us Weekly*, *People*, *Success*, and *Entrepreneur*, and her products can be found all over the nation at various retailers, big and small, as well as appearing often on primetime QVC. Jen has also already become a regularly featured business and lifestyle expert for such programs as FOX News' *Strategy Room*, ABC's *Money Matters*, CBS' *Early Show*, FOX Business News' *Your Money, Your Questions*, CNBC's *Big Idea with Donny Deutsch*, and Meredith Corporation's *Better TV*, and is a business contributor to *The Huffington Post*.

Jen's diverse experience, unique perspective, and knowledge enable her to identify with, relate to, motivate, and inspire people of varying backgrounds and demographics and have led her to become a highly sought-after speaker and author, contributing editorial pieces to several prominent business magazines and booking speaking engagements that include political conferences, charity fundraisers, Learning Annex seminars, and women's leadership conferences. She is also the National Spokesperson for Girls Take Charge, a leadership organization for girls nine to eighteen years of age, an organization where she also sits on the Board of Directors.

As a serial entrepreneur and small business advocate whose guidance and support have impacted thousands of business owners, Jen recently created and hosts Launchers Café, a cutting-edge entrepreneurial, multimedia, and interactive site with tens of thousands of members that is changing the way entrepreneurs learn, share information, and accelerate business growth.

Women's causes are paramount to Jen, as well. She has received numerous accolades and honors from women's organizations such as the Momentum Award from Ceslie Network/Ceslie.com recognizing her as one of the best and brightest women in business. Jen was also a nominee for an EWomen Network's International Femtor Award. Most recently Jen is the 2009 Honoree for the Women's

Venture Fund for her prominent work in being a role model and advocate for female entrepreneurs.

Jen Groover is simply a successful and balanced businesswoman who refuses to pick one box to fit into and instead thrives in all of them. Her religion is that of inspiration, creativity, and perseverance, and it is reflected in her mantras "Have more fear or regret than failure" and "What if . . . ? and Why not . . . ?" Find Jen online at www.jengroover.com and www.whatifandwhynot.com.